Freedom One Step at a Time

ISBN 978-1-68570-632-6 (paperback)
ISBN 978-1-68570-633-3 (digital)

Christian Faith Publishing
832 Park Avenue
Meadville, PA 16335
www.christianfaithpublishing.com

Printed in the United States of America

To those who, like me, want more of Thee…

Contents

Preface

In my personal never-ending search for more of Jesus Christ, more understanding of His Word, and certainly more understanding of myself, the Lord started me on a quest that I literally felt compelled to write into a book. It is my hope that these findings can be of aid and of comfort to other searching souls, as it has been for me.

Out of private prayer, the Lord spoke to me and said that if I wanted to know more about myself, then I must learn of His Jews and the people that surrounded them in their pilgrimage to the promised land. What followed was a fascinating discovery of priceless pearls in my life. For the Lord opened up for me a truth that I have long searched for, which is giving me His restful peace within my own soul. Certainly, this search is a lifelong one, and I do not begin to imply that I have totally secured Canaan land in my own life. But certainly by the leadership and directorship of the Holy Spirit, my life is forever changed. And my soul is ever more coming under the authority of Jesus Christ. I consistently will myself to come under His authority.

As I began to research the different people and tribes that were involved with the Hebrews in this particular time period, several truths surfaced. I found that each biblical group of people represented a type of personality trait within my own soul. The trek to freeing ourselves of these types always lies in the power of Jesus Christ. My prayer is that the realization of soulish freedom becomes evident in all lives who seek it and that this book can aid a saint who, like me, never finds himself satisfied but always wants more of Jesus.

My heart is full of love to my husband, Charlie, for his direction and interest in my research and for his constant help in all other areas that gave me the time to write. My deepest thanks and appreciation to Anne Herman for her constant encouragement, editing, and time.

Introduction

Through the ages, mankind has desired to determine the where, when, and how of his origin going to great lengths to place himself in history. Now history itself is nothing more than data compiled by man from his own perspective, based on relatively few artifacts and discoveries, in an attempt to prove or disprove theories handed down from other historians who used the same procedure themselves. Our history books are filled with various opinions of man about particular periods of the world's timetable, which attempt to give credence to his own conclusions, many of which are based on conclusions drawn by other men before him. The befuddled historian grapples with alleged facts and comes to falsely based conclusions where conclusions were not possible.

Man, in his own intellect, never manages to establish his true beginning, always giving credit to some uncovered civilization or one that did not record its own history. This is because of the basic fallacy that it is possible to record history without the mention of our Creator. For there is truly only one history—His story, the truth of the creation of man by Almighty God and His plan for man to be redeemed unto Himself. History is the love story of God wooing His children back unto Himself, without coercing His creation to obey Him yet grieving when they do not. All the while, God knows that total obedience to Him means ultimate contentment and fulfillment for the creature. History is the story of the creature attempting to put himself above the Creator. The only correct history there is, is the history written by divine instruction of the Holy Spirit (2 Timothy 3:16). The only valid history book is the Bible. Secular scholars constantly show amazement when any findings line up with the Bible, while in reality, we should be amazed that they don't begin with the Bible for direction in archeological searches.

God created the first man, Adam. Adam was made in the image of God Himself. Before the fall, Adam was a highly intelligent human being, completely free at this time from sin, thus functioning from a clear, alert mind with direct access to the living God. He walked with God in the cool of the evenings and conversed freely with the Creator who had made all things out of nothing (Hebrews 11:3). Adam's knowledge exceeded anything we could comprehend today. Consider the task of naming, not to mention remembering, all the names of all the animals (Genesis 2:19–20).

When Adam and Eve disobeyed God by eating of the fruit of the tree of knowledge of good and evil, sin entered into the world, and God was forced to expel them both not only from the garden of Eden but also from the presence of our perfect heavenly Father. There is no indication that Adam's God-given knowledge was taken away from him upon expulsion. Certainly, man's lifestyle altered drastically, but man did not then degenerate into apelike beings, forgetting all that God had spoken to him. At Adam's fall, man makes the decision to go it alone without the direction of his Creator, going his own way rather than the way God ordained for him. Surely, Adam must have experienced anguish and complete and utter heartbreak at what he had allowed to happen, not only to himself but also to all his descendants. But the Bible is God's story, and we are given few facts concerning Adam and his innermost thoughts. Immediately upon expulsion, God gave man the promise that, in spite of his disobedience, His plan had not nor would not change (Genesis 3:15). God desires fellowship with man and would bring perfect union about through Jesus Christ, the Son of God, the Redeemer of mankind.

Let us look for a moment at the cause of Adam's fall. By investigation, we can see our own innate sin of love of self. In Isaiah 64:9, God says He is the potter, and we are the clay, and so shall it always be. This truth has caused man to continuously clash with God, for man himself wants to be god. We do not want to accept the fact that we are clay, ever were clay, that surely now we have bettered ourselves into something too important and valuable to be in total submission to a Creator. And so secular historians consistently write history from the viewpoint that man has vastly improved his lot, bettered himself, increased his intellect, and in fact should be in control of his own destiny, to do not only as he sees fit but to put it more bluntly, take over the godship for himself.

To give an example, we can look at our culture today in regard to our legal system. By ignoring God's laws on finality of right and wrong, we have distorted eternal truths. Consequently, today, wrong is accepted as right, and right is accepted as wrong depending on the whim and mood of public opinion. Absolutes are considered narrowness of thought, and pseudointellectualism has distorted our moral fiber. Criminals who are actual threats to our very safety and life are free to not only roam the streets but to abuse the innocent and the righteous with absolutely no fear of any consequences, and few such offenders are brought to justice. To mention another example, homosexuality should not be considered a preference; the Word of God declares it is wrong. It is not an alternate lifestyle; it is sin. It is not to be accepted nor excused; it is wrong. Homosexuality is an abomination to God Almighty (Leviticus 18:22).

We shall never change God's laws without reaping the consequences. We reap what we sow. In the end, the consequences are always the same. We shall lose life, liberty, and happiness, for God is life, liberty, and happiness.

In Daniel 12:4, we are told that at the end of time, prior to second coming of our Lord Jesus Christ, knowledge, not necessarily wisdom, shall be increased. In light of such a prophecy, it is fascinating to note that it wasn't until the mid-1800s that archeologists discovered the earliest known civilization—that of the Sumerians. The Sumerians were located near the biblical garden of Eden close to the Tigris and Euphrates rivers. The discovery of Sumer, a highly civilized society, after 5,800 years under layers and layers of earth, was a very exciting find. It places biblical earth age at about 6,000 years old, contrary to secular dating. These findings are examples that validate Daniel's prophecy of increased knowledge at end-times, for this civilization has laid hidden for 5,800 years, only to be discovered in the last 130 years.

It is true that man's knowledge has increased just as the prophet Daniel predicted it would at the end of this age prior to the second coming of the Lord Jesus Christ. Our knowledge being increased is one thing, but the increase of our intellect is another. If anything, man has lost intelligence. Sin begets sin, and passing centuries of sin have only caused man to become more flawed in his thinking. In fact, if God, in His omnipotence and goodness, had not periodically breathed His breath of life across mankind throughout the ages, surely there would be no mankind for Him to redeem at all.

Consider the following: Where man exists, man worships. And how, what, and who man worships shapes not only the entire destiny of that particular man but his family, his community, his nation, and ultimately planet earth. Look at man without God. We need not dwell here on the heinous acts of so-called civilized man to see ourselves in reality. The ego that was expelled from the garden of Eden is the same perverted ego that today wants his own way, claims that man can improve his lot, and is good left unto himself. But it just isn't true. Even those who refute the truth of the Bible need only read secular history to see the unchanged degeneracy of man. There is no other power so destructive and so full of hatred and cruelty as man.

No bounds are considered sacred if they interfere with our desires. We abort the unborn of our own kind if they interfere with or don't fit into our plans, while at the same time, we pass laws to protect the lives of seals and snail darters. We indulge in sexual acts if it pleases the flesh and ignore any sense of righteous morality. We neglect our responsibility as parents and expect the state to raise our young people into citizens who will perpetuate our comfortable way of life. Our welfare system encourages people not to work. Honesty and the work ethic are being ridiculed while slothfulness and the sluggard are being supported and paid for by government. We worship materialism and expect a central government to take care of all our worldly desires. We teach humanism as our religion, denying godly principles of law and order. Many are aware of America's ills and see her impending death. Yet in the midst of all of these obvious failures, man continues to claim he is improving himself and is far above and superior to his six-thousand-year-old cousin, the Sumerian.

Man is a three-part creature: flesh, soul, and spirit. The spirit man yearns for fulfillment just as much as, in fact even more than, the soul and flesh of man. Since sin entered man and his descendants through the fall of Adam, there has existed within the spirit of man a vacuum that can only be filled by God's indwelling spirit. Man can and does attempt to fill this vacuum in many different ways, but only those people who come back to their Creator find the answer to their search for meaning in life.

To be born again is to accept Jesus Christ as your own personal Savior. At acceptance and repentance, the Holy Spirit then abides within the believer, and a new creature is in existence (2 Corinthians 5:17). Even then, the Christian sins. The only remedy for sin is repentance from the heart; that is, the admittance of wrongdoing for selfish reasons and prideful exaltation. Repentance then, by definition, is difficult for fallen man. Instead of seeking the one and only God and facing and admitting his sinful nature, man attempts to substitute every known alternative. He creates his own religions that focus on the desire for money, personal power, success, prestige, gain, and anything that exalts and supports self.

His gods are like man himself, full of faults, shortcomings, jealousies, and pride. His gods cheat, murder, lie, steal, commit every sexual perversion known unto man. Man can manipulate his gods. But open repentance, acknowledgement of sin, dying to self—this man rejects. Man rejects in his own nature the God of love who gives all and asks for nothing but to reside within the vessel He Himself created. This is God's grace, a truth about which volumes have been written but few ever understand in this life. We shall not attempt to expound upon the subject of grace here. To the born-again, it is life; to the unbeliever, it is folly.

Man then not only is a sinner by nature, a creature who delights in choosing his desire over the commandments of God, but man also has outside forces that seek to aid him in being separated from God's love and direction. The outside force is Satan and his evil angels, spirits, and demons (Ephesians 6:12). Satan, himself a fallen creature, fully understands man with his consuming pride and self-love. What Satan cannot understand is God's love for man. But if man is that important to God, then he is important to Satan.

Our Sumerian brother was fully aware of satanic forces. Continual sin has blocked out the perception of Satanic forces in modern society. Modern man has been so duped that, except for a minority of Christians, Satan is denied existence at all. This, no doubt, is Satan's greatest ploy and advantage against mankind: he does not exist; he can do no havoc. Denying Satan's existence is considered by modern man to be greatly enlightened. He then attributes all evil to God if he chooses to believe there is one. I Peter 5:8.

Once again, man's conclusions are wrong. The Bible states correctly that indeed there is a Satan, and his entire thrust is to attempt to prevent man from that supreme fellowship with his God. During the past millennia, Satan, being more intelligent than man, has successfully deceived God's creatures by appealing to our innate fallen nature—our pride. Surely, we think sophisticated, intellectual, learned twenty-first century man does not have to concern himself with an evil being. This attitude and belief portrays man's ultimate ignorance. Now Satan, totally hidden, can continue with his plan of setting himself up as ruler and dictator of the entire world. As the world spirals toward its own destruction, caused totally by rebellion against God, Satan eagerly awaits his prey. But it is always to be remembered that history, once again is, His Story, will be exactly as the Creator spoke it to be.

All our brothers of antiquity recognized the existence of evil angels, evil spirits, and demons. Their religions are full of them. Trying to cope with evil and explain it outside of the biblical definition of sin has always caused great problems for man. Ancient man accepting the truth of Satan's existence, attempted to appease evil with his various rituals and taboos, involving the gods. Modern man, rejecting the truth of the existence of Satan, blames all his woes on society itself and attempts to legislate goodness. But if evil is evil, it can neither be appeased nor legislated; it must be forgiven and eradicated by the precious blood of Jesus Christ.

True, man is a majestic creation, a creation above all created beings; yet magnificent though he is, man erroneously worships himself. He becomes his own god, determined to live without the rules and guidelines that have been laid down for his benefit and ultimate survival. He refuses to accept that he is the created, not the Creator. But alas, man was created. Obedience to the Creator is mandatory, otherwise man's ideals, laws, and justice possess no rule of final authority. Good becomes bad, and bad becomes good with the whim of the times. Total corruption befalls any given society in due time, and civilizations give way to civilizations.

God's ultimate plan has never changed. He Himself is the authority of all in all. His created beings must be in subjection and obedience to God the Father. Rebellion has been the pattern of all the universe since before Adam's fall. But God's plan has never changed, and with the perfect absolute obedience of His Son, Jesus Christ, rebellion has forever been judged and placed under our Lord. Now as subjects, we must learn obedience against which we are inherently rebellious. God's plan is perfect order, perfect obedience, perfect rule, all encompassed in God's Son, the Redeemer, Jesus Christ. Praise God, it shall come to pass, just as He has spoken it.

Chapter 1

The Sumerians

There is a correlation between the Jew and his pilgrimage to the promised land and the committed Christian and his pilgrimage to the abundant life and the inheriting of the kingdom of God in the now. God uses the physical life of the Jew to show us our inner and outer walk with Him. If we understand Jewish beginnings and their progress in its very particular order, we then see the order that our walk must occur and the order in which God deals with our flesh, soul, and spirit. Consequently, what shall be discussed is God's dealing with man from Eden to the choosing of Abraham and the outcome of his descendants in regard to their possession of the promised land. The habits, customs, and cultures of the Babylonians, Assyrians, and Egyptians shall be looked at in relation to their importance in our discussion of the inner soul of man. For there is indeed an inner story as well as an outer one. God, with His infinite knowledge, has a multitude of teachings and truths within the Bible and within the same material.

We will follow Abraham and his descendants from Babylonia, to Canaan, to Egypt, back to Canaan, ending with captivity in Babylonia again, and the return to Canaan before the diaspora. To capsule Israeli history, God called Abraham (Abram) from Ur in Babylonia. Abraham, the father of the Jews, came into Canaan land (the promised land) under God's direction. Four generations later, a famine took place in Canaan, forcing Abraham's descendant,

Jacob and his family, to flee to Egypt. They remained there and four hundred years passed before the Jews were freed from Egyptian slavery. After spending an additional forty years in the desert, they then returned to the promised land, only to find the land inhabited by numerous tribes. To reenter Canaan, the land had to be taken by force. The Jews were victorious, and a Jewish nation was established for a short time. But due to series of internal struggles, Israel was beset by civil war, and two nations emerged. The nation became divided into Israel in the North and Judah in the South, the division eventually weakened the Jews, and once again, they found themselves in foreign captivity. Southern Israel Judah, was taken captive by the Babylonians for a period of seventy years; Northern Israel was taken captive by the Assyrians. After seventy years in Babylon, the Jews returned home to rebuild Jerusalem. Once again, Israel was a nation for a short period of time. She remained loosely intact until the final scattering of the Jews, The Diaspora, took place after Rome destroyed Jerusalem in AD 70. Canaan land was not inhabited by the Jews as a nation again until the reestablishment of the modern-day state of Israel in 1948.

Our attention is focused on that time period from the original call to Abraham (Abram) in the city of Ur in Babylonia to the end of the second captivity by the Babylonians and Assyrians. The history is only mentioned briefly because the thrust of our interest lies in how the outer story of the Jew relates to our inner story as Christians. For there is a parallel for us as Christians in the spirit as we follow the Jews and their happenings in the flesh. It is this inner story that we will study.

After Adam and Eve's expulsion from the garden of Eden, children were born. With man living hundreds of years, population growth was no problem. The knowledge of God was taught from generation to generation, for a knowledge of God is evident in Adamic posterity, the Sumerians.

The Sumerian civilization was not unearthed or recognized by archeologists as a separate civilization until the mid 1800s, A.D. The discovery of these people substantiates, Daniel's prophecy of end-time increased knowledge. It was a sovereign act of God for a civilization to remain hidden for over 5,800 years until His choosing.

Sumer was situated by the biblical garden of Eden near the Tigris and Euphrates rivers. She began to decline around 2800 BC with the rise to power of the Babylonians and Assyrians. Sumer, the outgrowth of Adam and his descendants, was a very civilized society. But because of man's fallen nature, we have been taught falsely and readily accepted that we have improved ourselves through the millennia. The Sumerians however were a people quite like ourselves.

Sumerian technology included the potter's wheel, wheeled vehicles, sailboats, seed plows, writing, language, art (statues, plaques, friezes), music (harps and lyres), weaving, glassmaking, irrigation, and in fact, everything that is necessary for the perpetuation of a civilization. Their cuneiform writing became more exact and sophisticated as it became necessary with the growth of population and distances between people. In other words, man was not a cave dweller shouting ug-a-lugs to one another but, on the contrary, was ingenious at adapting and innovating what he needed. As Sumerian civilization grew, it is believed that there were existing at least twelve city-states with large populations before the Noahic flood.

Man left the garden of Eden with knowledge gained by walking with God Himself (Genesis 2). It should not be surprising to find a people such as the Sumerians and realize how advanced they were as a culture. For man did not immediately degenerate upon expulsion from the garden into beings with no head knowledge. What happened to man due to sin was a lack of conscience in doing right or the will of God. Now forevermore, man would be confronted with his will in conflict with the will of God until the second coming of Jesus Christ.

Man, in his fallen state, turned from his Creator. God tells us in Romans chapter 1 that all men are given a conscience and that no man is without the knowledge that he is a spiritual creature as well as a flesh creation. But man turned from God and His calling because he desired to do so, just as rebellion in us today is there, because we prefer our way to His way. Though we most assuredly live today in the dispensation of grace, sin and rebellion shall be dealt with and totally destroyed. God's judgment against the rebellious Sumerians was a flood. The forewarning of Noah was totally ignored, thus man suffered and died for his disbelief.

After the Noahic flood, Noah and his descendants again populated the area around the Tigris and Euphrates rivers. These people also referred to themselves as Sumerians, and it is from their cuneiform writings that we have learned much information about their history. These cuneiform tablets miraculously have been preserved for over forty-five hundred years. Even today, they are not brittle nor easily broken. In Sumerian archeological findings, such subject matters as the creation of the universe and man, the acknowledgment of the creative power of the divine Word (thus knowledge of God Himself), insights on sufferings, submission, death, and hell were all written about. The great flood also is referred to. Their writings indicate that the Sumerians were aware of a possible personal relationship with God. Generation upon generation obviously had shared such truths from the expulsion of Adam to their present time. It was natural that these things would be written about.

References also are found in their cuneiform writings, dealing with the tower of Babel and the scattering of man throughout the earth. It was at this time that the Sumerian civilization began to give way to the rise of the Babylonians and Assyrians, which in turn fragment off into a multitude of tribes, various cultures, and groups according to the Word of God. God had ordained for man to inhabit and occupy the earth to scatter himself abroad (Genesis 9:1).

The tower of Babel was built in direct disobedience to the Word of God. Man's sin and drive to be god himself continuously separates him from God.

> And they said, Go to, let us build us a city and
> tower, whose top may reach unto heaven, and let
> us make us a name lest we be scattered abroad
> upon the face of the whole earth. (Genesis 11:4)

The ziggurat, a tower, was built. The ziggurat was the sacred temple that the Sumerians used to house their gods. The architectural design of a ziggurat was the idea of a house up on a mountain. Built either rectangular or in a square, the structure diminishes in area as it increases in height, being built in three to seven stages. Plant life grew around each terrace, and all efforts were made to support the sacred shrine in hopes of visitation from a particular deity. The hope of building such a ziggurat to heaven, and hoping for visitation from a false god, was an abomination to God.

> And the Lord came down to see the city and tower, which the children of men builded. And the Lord said, Behold, the people are one, and they have all one language; and this they begin to do: and now nothing will be restrained from them, which they have imagined to do. Go to, let us go down, and there confound their language, that they may not understand one another's speech. So the Lord scattered them abroad from thence upon the face of all the earth: and they left off to build the city. Therefore is the name of it called Babel; because the Lord did there confound the language of all the earth: and from thence did the Lord scatter them abroad upon the face of all the earth. (Genesis 11:5–9)

With the diversity of languages and the scattering of the Sumerians, the civilization began to decline. The Babylonians and Assyrians rose to power. With the introduction of various languages, cultural differences became prevalent, and a number of cultures and heritages began to coexist throughout the earth. As new civilizations arose, they absorbed past cultures and incorporated parts of their heritages as well. With the rise of the Babylonian and Assyrian empires, there came great diversity of written languages also. The fall of the tower of Babel was in the past, and these two great empires vied for power over a period of about three thousand years. Another neighboring empire growing up on the Nile River was Egypt, which was populated with descendants of Ham, a child of Noah's.

As it was with the Sumerians, these people of the Fertile Crescent area were believers in numerous gods and felt the gods must be appeased in order for life to continue. There was a strong belief in demons and omens. The people's daily lives were full of taboos and rituals. Each locale would have many temples where the inhabitants would begin their day in worship. Religion was an integral part of man's life.

We can see that humanism took root in man with Adam upon leaving the garden of Eden and has been a growing cancer ever since. For from the beginning, sin has caused man to worship himself and disobey God's principle. His religions are filled with demonic activity and self-satisfaction. Still today, man's base nature consumes him, and many of his sins find their roots in sex and all its perversions. These, in turn, manifest themselves and erode every facet of life, robbing him not only of possible eternal life but of life abundant in the here and now under the direction and rulership of our sovereign God.

Man's gods were appeased in different forms and fashions. Celebrations, festivities and rites were focused on fertility and pro-creation. Even today, people are still consumed with sex, battling in courts over the right of abortions and homosexuals. But God's laws are never changing, though continually ignored. Sex and its numerous perversions are as old as the walk out of the garden, no less abhorrent to God but nevertheless present. Because man is the only creation that can be redeemed, what man does with sex and the procreation of his own kind is very important to God.

God gave us the power to recreate our own kind. Because only man can be redeemed, then what we create (our children) is redeemable. We have the capacity to create a being that will live forever. This is an awesome truth. The Bible tells us that our flesh will change with the coming of Jesus but that our spirits and souls live forever.

> Behold, I show you a mystery; We shall not all
> sleep, but we shall all be changed, In a moment,
> in the twinkling of an eye, at the last trump: for
> the trumpet shall sound, and the dead shall be

raised incorruptible, and we shall be changed. For this corruptible must put on incorruption, and this mortal must put on immortality. So when this corruptible shall put on incorruption, and this mortal shall have put on immortality, then shall be brought to pass the saying that is written, Death is swallowed up in victory. The sting of death is sin; and the strength of sin is the law. (1 Corinthians 15:51–56)

Whether we live in heaven or hell is our choice but that we live forever is a choice already made by our Creator. All who have lived, are living, or will live are preordained by God Himself to exist forever. Forever is a concept we can only speak of; understanding is beyond our comprehension at this time.

God gave us the family and the laws for its order. We have ignored these laws and rebelled just as we have rebelled against all other things of God. But here we are dealing with something that is unique—forever beings, everlasting creations; the Creator spoke it to be.

All our brothers of antiquity recognized the existence of evil angels, evil spirits, and demons. Their religions are full of such. Trying to cope with evil and explain it outside of the biblical definition of sin has always caused great problems for man. Ancient man, accepting the truth of Satan's existence, attempted to appease evil with his various rituals and taboos involving the gods. Modern man, rejecting the truth of the existence of Satan, blames all his woes on society itself and attempts to legislate goodness. But if evil is evil, it can neither be appeased nor legislated; it must be forgiven and eradicated by the precious blood of Jesus Christ.

No civilization has lasted throughout all of world history because all man has mocked God. Neither nations nor individuals can ignore God's eternal principles and continue to exist. Sowing and reaping are eternally in effect. Man has not improved; in fact, he has degenerated because of the literal piling on of sin upon sin. Yet in our culture and heritage, in our learned background, the idea that we have improved ourselves is ingrained in each of us, and this thought is responsible for the tremendous growth of humanism in America today. For again, we believe that we can improve ourselves by our technological advances, medical achievements, and cultural and educational programs. The spirit of man, the inner man and his hunger for righteousness and for cleanliness, is ignored by man himself. However, none of these things alter the plan of Almighty God. His unchangeable laws confront our wills on every turn. We, as a people, attempt to replace God with our own gods. We today, as Americans, have gone whoring after two main gods—humanism and materialism. Carnal Christians dabble in Christianity and attempt to separate it from their daily lives, hence the term Sunday Christians. But the spiritual Christian desires to practice his Christianity in the midst of his daily routine. Jesus is the integral part of his life, the entire focal point for existence. Again, whatever we worship, we spend time with. As time is spent with God, the life takes on the character of God or of any god worshipped for that matter. For the devout believer, to be like Him is life. For the carnal Christian, compromise, leavening, and a shared will with God are ways of life. The old commercial, "a little dab will do you," is the premise that carnal Christians cling to. This attitude again is as ancient as the thoughts and attitudes of the Sumerians.

Our own culture lies in peril today as we find the same problems besetting us as beset our ancient cousins. Our separation from God and playing religion has caused corruption in every area of our lives that, without a miracle from God Himself, America too is doomed to disappear along with all past civilizations of world history. And so mystical Babylon, the social order of the world based on money, power, and prestige, is more entrenched than ever. Yet in spite of social evolutionists' pro arguments, the truth is that the world is not getting better, and neither is man. On the contrary, mankind is as depraved as ever. The United States, with all its multitudes of problems, is still the best country in the world to live in, yet it too along with the entire world order appears to be on the verge of collapse. Both secular and biblical scholars agree on this point. Every aspect of our lives lies in peril—economically, socially, and especially spiritually.

Chapter 2

The Background

God's plan has never changed for man. From the beginning, with the formation of the earth, God has consistently had His plan unfolding. Sumer gave way to the Babylonians and Assyrians by turning away from God, and ultimately, she fell as a civilization. Man refused to govern himself according to his conscience, which God placed inside of him, continuing to place himself above all else. This attitude is what brought about judgment and the flood. Yet no sooner was man back upon the ground than sin became rampant again. God (remembering His plan has never changed) chose not to draw the entire rebellious human race to Himself. He chose rather to show Himself through a people He had selected. To these people only, at this time in world history, would God reveal Himself. And through these chosen people, He would show the world that He is truly the one and only God.

From the Fertile Crescent, the hotbed of civilization, God called forth a man, named Abram whom God would rename Abraham and from this man, He built Himself a people different from all peoples of the world. More importantly, from this man came the continuous unbroken line that produced the mother of the Savior of mankind. Abram was the son of a father whose business was the making of idols to sell. Yet Abram heeded the voice of God and obeyed His calling. God called Abram out from among his own people and gave him the promise that he would become the father of many nations.

> Now the Lord had said unto Abram, Get thee
> out of thy country, and from thy kindred, and
> from thy father's house, unto a land that I will
> show thee: And I will make of thee a great nation,
> and I will bless thee, and make thy name great;
> and thou shalt be a blessing: And I will bless
> them that bless thee, and curse him that curseth
> thee: and in thee shall all families of the earth be
> blessed. (Genesis 12:1–3)

> And I make thy seed as the dust of the earth: so
> that if a man can number the dust of the earth,
> then shall thy seed also be numbered. (Genesis
> 13:16)

With the coming forth of Abram, (Abraham), the Jew made his debut upon world history, and history was never again the same. Nothing can or does happen hereafter that does not, in some way, involve the Jew and the land that God Himself stated He would give to the people He chose out of the world—the Jewish (Jewish people), the people of the future nation of Israel.

> In the same day the Lord made a covenant with
> Abram, saying, Unto thy seed have I given this
> land, from the river of Egypt, unto the great river,
> the river Euphrates. (Genesis 15:18)

To the secular student, Israel is indeed a constant befuddlement because such a small minority of people and trivial piece of real estate in apparent desolation hold such importance on the world scene. It appears the Jew constantly causes wrath, jealousy, and turmoil wherever he is. Even the Jew himself has been confused as to his role in the world, hearing he is God's chosen but not understanding the plan of God. For, as a nation, the eyes of Israel are yet blinded to the truth of Jesus Christ. But to the believing student of God, the Jew is God's reality, the fulfillment of His prophecies, the assurances of God's promises, the perfect timetable to watch as planet Earth rolls down its clock and ends this final age prior to the second coming of our Lord and Savior Jesus Christ. Ah, the Jew, he is beloved by the Christian. He tells our story in the flesh. As we follow his walk, we can see ourselves in our walk in the Spirit. To know the Jew is to know ourselves. For God tells and shows us through the Old Testament the story of the Jews and thus the story of ourselves as we walk to the cross and into the mature Christian life.

Out of the midst of the sin and idol worship, God called Abram. So it is with us. Into our lives, God reaches down. And in the midst of all of our sins and out of all the sea of humanity, He calls us forth. As it was with the flesh of Abram, so it is with the spirit of us who hear God's call. We come to Him and are born again. As Abram left Babylon, it appeared that he had left behind all of his heritage. All those things that could or would beset him seemed to be in the past. So it is with us when we first meet Jesus Christ and are born again; all of our problems and those things that beset us seem to disappear. Like the people of the Fertile Crescent tended to blend together into one, so it is with us as people. The facets of our personalities seem at last to blend together, and we feel integrated for the first time. No longer fragmented and filled with inner turmoil and problems, we now have exchanged those feelings for peace and love. Our walk with the Lord Jesus Christ is in a honeymoon period. This honeymoon period changes as we grow in the Spirit. Our relationship and love of God is no less real with the passing of time; in fact, it is more enriching. But just as there are growths and steps in a marriage, so it is with our walk with God.

The Babylonian and Assyrian empires were made up of a mixture of people, each group distinct unto itself but living within the empires. Babylonia and Assyria swapped power back and forth during this time in ancient history. Each empire had its own characteristics. Both were sinful empires; neither were pleasing to God. Yet the difference for us to see here as Christians is significant, for there is a type for us to notice here.

Whereas Assyria, by nature, was very warlike and interested in crushing all its foes and ruling unmercifully, Babylonia was more peaceful and interested in tranquility and the pursuance of the better life. A similar comparison could be made between Sparta and Athens of antiquity or the United States and Russia of modern times. Where the Assyrians had much to say in their writings of their conquests and exploits, the Babylonians had little to say about military matters at all—in fact, the most complete report of a Babylonian military exploit in the Bible in their dealings with God's Jews.

The geography and location of the Fertile Crescent automatically produced a different breed of human behavior, not heathen in the sense of barbaric and wild as we have been erroneously taught, but mobile, more warlike in nature, and ever changing as myriads of peoples came across the flatlands of the Mesopotamian area. Remembered that though the area consisted of many groups, each people were distinct and different from one another. Each is an outgrowth of the tower of Babel experience with their different languages and customs. Secular history has tended to group all of these ancient peoples together. This is not a true picture. Much can be learned from the different natures of these people, and it is here that our interest lies. For it is in the interwoven story of the Jew and his relationship in the flesh to the people of Mesopotamia that we can see ourselves in the Spirit.

A third empire ruling at this time was Egypt, the princess of the Nile, descendants of Noah's son, Ham: "Israel also came into Egypt, and Jacob sojourned in the land of Ham" (Psalm 105:23). The Egyptian empire was certainly prospering at this time. Egypt was a highly cultured, learned, unwarlike society. In fact, there was a great deal of order within this empire in contrast to the constant sweeping changes of peoples and customs in the Mesopotamian area. The people themselves were content to live out their lives within the borders of Egypt. Everyday life, even for the lower classes, was quite pleasant. Women were highly respected as it was from the female that the monarchial linage was established. Egyptian women spent as much time in dress and makeup as their modern Western counterpart. The term "worldly" would indeed be applicable to the Egyptian culture.

Ancestor worship did plague the society. It was believed by early Egyptians that dead pharaohs continued to rule from their graves along with the reigning pharaoh. The pharaohs were considered to be gods, thus great concern for the Egyptian afterlife consumed the present life of each ruling king as well as many officials. But even though burial tombs and pyramids dotted the landscape, the people themselves were not totally consumed with death. Theft of burial grounds was a great problem, and many vocations were involved in the building and reparation of the grave sites. The engineering feat of the Egyptian pyramid is still very much applauded today. As we study the Egyptian, we find that with the exception of technological advancements, these people are very much like us. We are not nearly more sophisticated as we like to believe.

God had a purpose and plan in choosing Abram (Abraham) from Ur of the Babylonian Empire rather than from the Egyptian Empire. Egypt is protected from outsiders by the Nile River and her vast dessert. Her separateness enabled her to establish her culture and customs without interference from outsiders. Natural geography separated Egypt and her people in such a way that it enabled her culture to be distinct and different from the other civilizations of the world of antiquity. For within the Fertile Crescent (Babylonian/Assyrians empires), all people appeared to be a conglomeration of multicultures, not separate at all. The very reason God did not choose an Egyptian was because Egypt was already separated. God showed that He needs no natural or earthly phenomena to bring about "separateness." He Himself brings forth a people and then makes them "peculiar". Deuteronomy 14:2

> But ye are a chosen generation, a royal priesthood, a holy nation, a peculiar people; that ye should show forth the praises of him who hath called you out of darkness into his marvelous light: Which in time past were not a people, but are now the people of God: which had not obtained mercy, but now have obtained mercy. (1 Peter 2:9–10)

We too, as Abrams, are born again as Abraham. And we too, as born-again believers, enter into the promised land. We have eternal life and can begin to experience life abundantly. But in order to secure the promised land in our own lives, we must not only have a born-again and a Pentecost experience but also determine in our own hearts to make Jesus Christ the author and finisher of our faith. Even as Pentecost Christians, those baptized in the Holy Spirit, there is yet so much more with Jesus. We seek Him and lay down our will for His will in our lives. After a period of time, as it is with any father-child relationship, God expects and desires for us to begin to mature. Knowing Him is obeying Him, and this takes maturity. Many Christians do not wish to mature at all prefer to remain babes without growth or experience.

Certainly, God's plan is for us to be His children, but He also desires for us to be brothers and sisters of Jesus Christ and to inherit what He has for us. However maturity is mandatory, not only because it is pleasing to God, which should be sufficient, but also because there is much for us as we grow up into our salvation. This growth brings about the inheritance of the abundant life here on earth. It is God's desire to see His Word manifested in our lives, and we learn His Word as we walk the road of experience. But as it is with any small child, we must be pushed. Abraham was pushed out of the promised land due to a famine. He was moving into a deeper dimension with God, and many times we find ourselves in a very dry place first, then the work in our innermost being begins. We must come out of our initial euphoria with God. The honeymoon period ends where all prayers are instantly answered, and all problems seem to disappear. For if all prayers are answered, all problems are solved without any effort or diligence on our behalf, then we exist contrary to God's ultimate plan for our lives. We must hunger for God's Word before we shall seek it. We must be driven into His Word, for left alone, we are lackadaisical and totally undisciplined.

God's desire for us is to be like His Son, Jesus, in every way; therefore, we must be taught obedience just as His Son was taught obedience. Obedience is learned through trials, tribulations, sufferings, and a disciplined life. Its reward is a life full of the Son, His character, His righteousness, and His precious grace.

The famine forced Abraham's descendants to Egypt. A famine for the lack of God's Word in our lives forces us too into a new direction. For many Christians, the road ends here; salvation is secure, and a deeper walk is not sought. God continues to love and draw these people to Him, but the overcoming life has been denied by the Christian himself. Others greatly hunger, and the famine makes way for this insatiable appetite to be filled in a faith walk as yet unseen or known but yearned for nevertheless. Their very lack becomes their blessing, for to be filled becomes a drive in itself. This believer seeks God and evermore seeks Him.

Chapter 3

Egypt and the Flesh

The Hebrews were at first guests in Egypt, then later became slaves. It was four hundred years before the Hebrews were freed from their captivity, but freed indeed they were. This too we should remember as we find ourselves in a trial or tribulation. Freed we shall become. It is patience we must learn, for God's Word will never fail us. He takes us into Egypt to free us from ourselves, "for in Him we live, and move, and have our being" (Acts 17:28). Our walk with the Lord takes on new depth as He begins that never-ending process of building character. In His likeness by manifold experiences, sufferings, trials, and tribulations, we see ourselves as we really are and become more like Jesus himself. For He comes to abide not only with us but within us as well.

Abide in me, and I in you. (John 15:4)

Before we are capable of seeing ourselves deep within, God must first free us from the outward, from the obvious, from Egypt. Perhaps this sounds simple, but again, to an unregenerated soul, this process is not easy. Our soul resides within His, along with the born-again spirit. Accepting Jesus Christ as the Son of God and being born again does not regenerate our souls. The regeneration of our soul is our maturation with Jesus Christ. We must renew our minds and souls by the Word of God and by walking through experiences. This is our life as believers on earth. We literally do grow up into our salvation.

> But speaking the truth in love, may grow up into
> him in all things, which is the head, even Christ.
> (Ephesians 4:15)

For the Gospel of Jesus Christ intends not only for us to enter into the kingdom of God but also to now inherit Him who is life and life more abundant.

> The thief cometh not, but for to steal, and to
> kill, and to destroy; I am come that they might
> have life, and that they might have it more abun-
> dantly. (John 10:10)

But to inherit what Jesus has for us is impossible without the power of the Holy spirit, for we can bring about no change within ourselves. Both the outward change and the inward change are accomplished by God Himself as we relinquish our will to Him.

Egypt is representative of the outward man, our flesh. She represents the order we think we have in our lives, the perfection we feel we have achieved, the facades we wear, and the things we do and say to protect our egos. Egypt is our lust for power, money, and prestige and acceptance. Egypt desired to separate herself from the rest of the world, claiming supremacy, and in the same way, we desire to separate ourselves from others around us claiming superiority. However, it is never what we have or do not have that concerns God and our relationship with Him but rather how we view what we have or do not have. For His desire is for us to overcome the world through Him, not have the world overcome us.

Egypt considered herself quite superior to the Babylonian and Assyrian empires. She took pride that the people of the Fertile Crescent came to her but seldom did her own people leave their boundaries for travel. Egypt strangles us and causes us to wear clothes and believe thoughts and react in programmed ways that eventually destroy the people we were meant to be. For as we travel through life, we truly become like the gods we serve. Egypt, or flesh, is worshipped, and her participants become like her. The believer never becomes better or improves his flesh with time in Egypt; he only becomes worse and eventually reaps what has been sown. The Egyptian way of life appeals to our sinful nature and our lustful egos. To cheat, manipulate, social climb, and put ourselves first while hiding behind pseudorighteousness is appealing to our base nature. Egypt lures all men. And through the ages, Satan has enticed and captured humanity by every conceivable ploy known to mankind. Man is inevitably lured by power, money, and prestige.

Every man believes he can conquer Egypt, the flesh. Man believes he can improve himself by his own devices and wit. The flesh, however, is only overcome in knowing God Himself. Without God, many lay waste their entire lives, wandering around in the world's system, never conscious that there is another kingdom, never seeing the promised land of this life or the next, nor even realizing that it has been there all the time. Others, born-again but satisfied, remain in Egypt, also not understanding God's principles and being tossed to and fro, experiencing a life void of power and victory.

There is no difference here between ancient man and modern man. Though the description of the times may sound different, the Egyptian life portrays the same redundant pathetic scenario. For the ego with all its manifestations is the same ego within the Sumerian as it is within the American. From Nimrod to his modern counterpart, we can follow the steps of man and see his flesh or Egypt uncontrolled and outside the obedience of God, his Creator. Egypt lures man and slowly leavens him by her offer of power, prestige, and money.

A very upright, truly moral, educated individual awakes one morning in modern America to find himself miserable, lonely, and depressed. Social achievement within Egypt, the world's system, has proven to be a mirage. The flesh perhaps is somewhat satisfied, but the inner man is not. The more the individual feels he has attained what he has worked for, the emptier it now seems. The individual looks for bigger thrills within Egypt. With each of life's gaps being filled with greater promised thrills, the reality of unfulfillment becomes all the more evident. The new house, the new car, the country club, the various trips, the job promotions are all exciting for a while yet still unable to fill the vacuum deep within. The ego is insatiable, and misery edges its way up into the consciousness of man. The nagging hole cannot be filled by the world's system. Oh man, only God can give what we so desperately need. And it is the opposite of what we think; rather than self-exaltation, completeness is found in self-denial and following Jesus Christ with all our heart. For the peace that passes all understanding lies in doing just the opposite of what the world calls us to do.

This lonely, depressed, empty individual finds himself in an unhappy marriage. The spouses feel deprived of the love they both need so badly. It had started out so good, but now the marriage is for all practical purposes over; when did it happen? The alcoholic executive, the drug-addicted housewife abetted by legally prescribed medicines, the hidden adultery, the lying that has become so necessary, constant game playing with only surface sharing, never heart-to-heart truths unless screamed in a rage, the disappointing children who had been given everything—suddenly life is in shambles. Oh, Egypt, it had all seemed so enticing. Where had it gone wrong?

These poor empty souls had been the high school kings and queens. Their classmates had elected them presidents of their fraternities and sororities, and the college had voted them most likely to succeed. Their early years of marriage had marked them for success and plenty of good times. These people were the style setters and had become part of America's power structure all over the country from large cities to small communities. Their names and pictures appear in the newspapers, especially in the business and society sections. Many politicians come from their ranks and are backed by each other's money. The social scene dances to their commands, and private, coveted clubs bulge from their membership. What happens in such lives?

These prima donnas do not appear as wicked people, in fact just the opposite. In American life, these people are considered the backbone of our society. They are willing to work for what they want and are always conscious of improving themselves and being able to offer a better life for their children. They are totally motivated by the American way of life. The Egyptian lure, however, never ends. Always they are interested in moving up and doing better, whatever better is. The values once possessed in the beginning of life's journey are now buried deeply in the many years of trying to conquer the unconquerable Egypt, the ever-yearning, never satisfied, flesh of man. It is man's continuous attempt to carve out his own image, to make himself god. But beneath the social veneer are hungry spirits camouflaged with the glitter and tinsel of the world.

Egypt is not the answer for man's yearning. It is a personal relationship with Jesus Christ that so many yearn for. Only in Christ is man able to forfeit Egypt and her constant call. With the fall of Adam, all descendants are in Adam's image or in the image of corrupted sinful man. Jesus Christ frees us in the spirit and cleanses us from all sin, but the flesh is forever doomed. When we reign with Jesus, we shall have new uncorrupted bodies.

> Behold, I show you a mystery; We shall not all sleep, but we shall all be changed, In a moment, in the twinkling of an eye, at the last trump: for the trumpet shall sound, and the dead shall be raised incorruptible, and we shall be changed. For this corruptible must put on incorruption, and this mortal must put on immortality. (1 Corinthians 15:51–53)

Our bodies in this world are corrupt and sinful by nature. But within the reborn are living spirits abiding with God Himself by the power of the Holy Spirit.

However, although we do abide in corrupted bodies there is no excuse for corrupted behavior. As Christians, we earnestly repent for every single action taken against God. Our thoughts are to be brought into the obedience of Jesus Christ. Corruption is not an excuse for our behavior. It is just a fact that we are by nature corrupt, all the more reason for our love for our Savior, Jesus Christ. He came, lived, died, and was resurrected. Without Him who is life, there is no life, for sin abounds unabated otherwise.

For the non-Christian, Egypt is not just a snare, it is ultimately death. For Egypt promises everything but gives nothing in return. She promises the love, adoration, and security that all human beings, since the time of Eden, have hungered for, which in reality can only be found in filling the vacuum with God Himself. Without a relationship with God, there is only sin upon sin.

> Woe to the rebellious children, saith the Lord, that take counsel, but not of me; and that cover with covering, but not of my spirit, that they may add sin to sin: That walk to go down into Egypt, and have not asked at my mouth; to strengthen themselves in the strength of Pharaoh, and to trust in the shadow of Egypt! (Isaiah 30:1–2)

Even for the born-again, the flesh must always be contended with. The flesh must be placed under the spirit. For many believers, the decision to leave Egypt is not made, and these believers live a leavened life, short of the victory that Jesus Christ has for His children. For those who are baptized in the Holy Spirit, there is a struggle always with Egypt too. Even for those who press on and on and choose to leave Egypt, it must be remembered that she is met again and again in our walk with the Lord. Past snares, having been overcome, arise periodically, and the wounds of the flesh are reopened. Once again, we can follow God's Jews in the flesh to understand ourselves in the spirit.

At the opening verses of the book of Exodus, (means departure) seventy Hebrews arrive in Egypt in order to avoid a famine in suffering Canaan. It appeared that because of the reigning position of Jacob's son, Joseph, the Jews would have no problem in Egypt. Yet the Jews remained in Egypt for four hundred years as slaves. It is the same with believers today; we erroneously feel we can conquer our flesh and control our own destiny. We dabble with the world, ignoring our own corruption and become slaves to the system we felt we could conquer. Egypt is never conquered; she must be left. Egypt is neither forgotten nor truly dead. Periodically, our flesh and all its ramifications will rise up to defeat us for a time and definitely cause us problems in our Christian walk. Just as the Jews and their captivity in Egypt represent our flesh and its captivity in the world, we learn that leaving Egypt and the world is a repetitious daily relinquishment of ourselves to the obedience of the Spirit of God. Victory over our flesh is found in repentance, not in good deeds! God assures us of the overcoming life found only in Him, not in ourselves, for we cannot be improved, only forgiven when we repent.

The social system of this earth is owned and controlled by the prince of this world, Satan himself. We cannot leave this earth, that is Egypt, unless we die. And our flesh, by biblical definition, is corrupt and not only enjoys but is comfortable in Satan's domain. Therefore, as Christians, there is that constant battle between the spirit and flesh. If the soul is not regenerated, the flesh will rule. Though the believer remains born again, any effective witness becomes impossible. Even a witness unto himself becomes ineffective. Though the believer is aware that he is born again, he is also very much aware of the defeated life he lives. A regenerated soul is the reward for the believer who chooses the overcoming life with Jesus Christ.

There is definitely a difference between the Christian who chooses Jesus Christ as Savior and the one who chooses Him both as Savior and Master. For the latter, the road continues to get more and more narow, and fewer and fewer travel upon it. This disciple must lay all at the feet of the Lord Jesus Christ. In order for this to happen, the Holy Spirit brings Him continuously into the image of Jesus Christ by experience upon experience of obedience. For this Christian, Egypt must be fought. There is a war between the flesh and the spirit (Romans chapter 8). This believer keeps himself in a penitent state of mind, depending not on his own resources but upon the Spirit of God. As soon as we believe we can do anything without God, we can rest assured we are planted in Egypt. To think we can accomplish things on our own is indicative that the flesh is busy at work. A busy flesh ignores the gentle spirit.

Disciples of Jesus Christ realize that it is through sufferings, tests, trials, and tribulations that we are made into His image and that our offerings cannot be compared to the glory we experience.

> For I reckon that the sufferings of this present time are not worthy to be compared with the glory which shall be revealed in us. (Romans 8:18)

So the road narrows for this believer. Things we could once do are no longer acceptable. Our likes and dislikes change. From where we were once comfortable, we find we must depart and not enter in. It is a slow process but real. And miraculously, none of the past is missed; perhaps remembered fleetingly as Satan stirs forgotten waters but never longed after. The choice has been made. The narrow road is chosen.

> Enter ye in at the strait gate: for wide is the gate, and broad is the way, that leadeth to destruction, and many there be which go in thereat: Because strait is the gate, and narrow is the way, which leadeth unto life, and few there be that find it. (Matthew 7:13–14)

Contentment begins to grow within us. Let such contentment never halt our growth so that we become content where we are with Him. For there is a vast difference in becoming content with where we are with Him and in becoming content with who we are in Him. In Him, we are becoming the empty vessels He has called us to be, not stupid and dulled into robots but alive and quickened by the Spirit of Almighty God. We move into the kingdom realm that the natural eye cannot behold. And every single solitary day becomes an adventure...we rejoice because we know Him. And life is our Creator dwelling within us by His Spirit! We no longer seek to exalt ourselves but seek to please and exalt the only one worthy of praise, our Father which art in heaven.

Chapter 4

The Babylonians and the Soul

Just as the Jews had to face Egypt, we too must face our flesh. But just as God freed His chosen people from the slavery of Egypt, He also frees us from the ownership of the world as we choose His Word over the desires of our flesh. God desired to place His nature into the nature of man, replacing the world in man with God in man. The Jew was established by God, calling out Abram from the bondage of Babylonia. Abram and his family went into the promised land. His descendants were forced into Egyptian captivity, which is symbolic of the corruption of the world and our flesh. The Christian can parallel his experience in the following manner. He too, before being born again, existed in Babylonia. Babylonia was the cradle of civilization. Man's history is in Babylonia, Sumer's descendants. Every other group of people have emerged from this area and spread throughout the world. This was the seat of mankind. Everything that man was—the world's corruption and man void of God—was in Babylonia.

Each person therefore has Babylonia within them. Our souls are full of Babylonian entrenchments: past events, memories, feelings, emotions, hurts, pride, triumphs, defeats, victories, failures, parental heritage, mores, folkways, culture, prejudices, traits, ideas, knowledge, human wisdom, and relationships. It is within the soul that we find our intellect, our emotions, and our will. Much, much healing is needed here. We have memories that beset us—incorrect concepts, imbedded cultural ties, and multitudes of wrong thought patterns that must come under the blood of Jesus. This, plus much more make up our personalities. Now in the flesh, Abraham came out of Babylonia and, before going into Egyptian captivity, was given the promised land. In the same manner, we as Christians leave Babylonia by being born again and come into the promised land of salvation. It appears to the Christian that all his problems are solved and that the Babylonian entrenchments are eradicated. The truth is, however, for a period of time, they have been overshadowed by the presence of Jesus Christ. Our personality problems are not healed. Our soul is still unregenerated as salvation does not regenerate the soul but sets the stage for regeneration to begin. The soul is regenerated by walking and living through the experiences of life with the power of Jesus Christ residing within the believer. This is accomplished by reading and studying the Bible and by repentance.

Salvation is given by grace and the heart belief that Jesus Christ is the Son of God. Sins are now forgiven for the asking, and repentance becomes a way of life. But there is so much more beyond salvation. If salvation were the total intent of God for our lives, then as soon as we were born again, we should hope to die and meet our Maker. But on the contrary, our lives just begin when we are born again. Jesus Christ equipped us for life here and, as He says, not just life but the abundant life. Without the baptism of the Holy Spirit, the abundant life is impossible. Yet even with the baptism of the Holy Spirit, our entire thrust in life must be to continue to move forward with Him. The Spirit does indeed lead us, and not only our flesh but our soul also must be willing to follow. The soul is a separate entity from the flesh, and it too must be changed by Jesus Christ. The flesh can be denied; the soul must be trained.

Remember, Egyptian captivity is symbolic of the flesh and the lust thereof and its pull toward the world. The Jew was freed from Egypt and returned to the promised land to find it was inhabited by numerous tribes. The different groups of people inhabiting the promised land at this time were not believers of God, nor did they desire to follow His ways. These people were enemies of God and thus enemies of the Hebrews, God's people. In the book of Joshua,

God commanded the returning Jewish tribe to destroy all adversaries they came up against in battle.

> And Joshua said, Hereby ye shall know that the living God is among you, and that he will without fail drive out from before you the Canaanites, and the Hittites, and the Hivites, and the Perizzites, and the Girgashites, and the Amorites, and the Jebusites. (Joshua 3:10)

Each of these tribes was also an outgrowth of the Babylonians who had migrated into the area of the promised land during the four-hundred-year absence of the Jews. The area was fully population by these tribes when the Jews returned. Both these people and the Hebrews were descendants from the Fertile Crescent area. The Babylonians traits, the sins of the world, existed in both the reigning tribes in the promised land and in the Jew attempting to return home. The difference in the Jew and the other tribes was the presence of God with the Hebrew. The only difference between Christians and non-Christians is the presence of God in the life of the Christian. The many tribes that resided in the promised land represented the same sins that were found in Babylonia. Man in Babylonia was not aware of his darkness, for he knew not God until God revealed Himself to man. Each of the tribes that inhabited the promised land had Babylonian natures. They were still in darkness, for they knew not God.

The Hebrew, upon returning to the promised land, faced in each tribe the same old nature that he thought he had left behind. In other words, our personalities have not changed with salvation. We are new creatures in Christ Jesus. But we must regenerate our souls to live the victorious life in Jesus Christ. The Jews captured Canaan land, and in the same way, we must overtake and capture our souls by allowing Jesus Christ to come in and destroy our Babylonian entrenchments.

The deep-seated sins in the personality of man are bound by an unregenerated soul. The takeover of the promised land portrays a type of man overcoming his own unregenerated soul by the power of the Holy Spirit. To summarize, to overcome Babylonian traits in Babylonia is impossible. Darkness prevails, and man is but a carnal creature living in sin. The flesh cannot improve the flesh. Even if man desired to improve himself, it is scripturally impossible. No one except Jesus Christ indwelling man can make him a new creature, enabling a permanent change. While man cannot better himself, his sinful traits can be overcome by walking with Jesus and possessing God's power within.

> With man it is impossible, but not with God; for
> with God all things are possible. (Mark 10:27)

The placing of the mind and the soul under the authority of Jesus Christ takes prayer without ceasing, for there is no leaving ourselves. Within our soul is our personality—the people we are. Our only recourse is more of Jesus. As we pour ourselves more into Him, we have more light in our lives. We obey ourselves into the light of the Gospel of Jesus Christ. Thus, if we do not know the Word of God, we cannot obey it. If we do not obey the Gospel, soul freedom is impossible. God is not just interested in having us become people of His in the eyes of the world; He desires for inward lasting changes within the believer himself. This change takes place as we read the Bible and learn of God. God's desire is to integrate our multifaceted personality under the dominion of Jesus Christ. The Babylonia within us, God will bring under the rulership of Jesus. We shall be integrated into one. Our souls shall no longer be unruly with thoughts that beset us and separate us from our Creator, but our minds and souls will discover disciplined order with Him who is both the order and Creator of all things. We memorize Scriptures and speak and do the Word by His power.

Flesh must first be recognized and dealt with before soulish captivity can be seen and understood. Recapturing the promised land is only an experience for those who first see Egypt the sins within them.

And I am come down to deliver them out of the
hand of the Egyptians, and to bring them up
out of that land unto a good land a large, unto
a land flowing with milk and honey; unto the
place of the Canaanites, and the Hittites, and the
Amorites, and the Perizzites, and the Hivites, and
the Jebusites. (Exodus 3:8)

Understand that our purpose here is to show how these tribes
are representative of the condition of our souls. Each one represents
a sin of our soul that must be overcome by the blood of Jesus Christ,
if it is to be overcome at all. This does not happen overnight any
more than Joshua defeated the Semitic groups in the promised land
overnight. God instructed Joshua to totally destroy the tribes; therefore, through the blood of Jesus Christ, victory is also available to the
believer. He is able to make definite changes in his personality and is
brought more into the image of Jesus Christ.

And how much healing is possible depends on how much
the believer yearn to die to self. There is a battleground that exists
within our souls. The Fertile Crescent area was a continuous battleground with hordes of different people tramping across its grounds.
Different tribes were rising and falling, moving about from one area
to another. So it is in our souls; the various traits that are carnal in
nature, not spiritual at all, haunt us and attempt to pull us away from
Jesus. Many times, our thoughts appear to trample across our souls,
leaving us battle-worn and fatigued. Old patterns are by far easier. It
is easy to remain what we have always been. It is easy to think how
we have always thought, but God calls us to act and think differently.
He tells us we must take the kingdom of God by force, training our
thoughts to be on Him and casting down those things that are not
aligned with His Word. We must pray that the Holy Spirit will reveal
to us our true carnal nature in order that all things be placed under
the dominion of Christ.

We cannot separate ourselves from the world; God must do it
through us, then we too, like Jesus, have overcome the world.

> But ye are a chosen generation, a royal priest-
> hood, a holy nation, a peculiar people; that ye
> should show forth his marvelous light: which in
> time past were not a people but are now the peo-
> ple of God: which had not obtained mercy, but
> now have obtained mercy. (1 Peter 2:9–10)

We sit in darkness, and He draws us to Him to free us from ourselves. For it is in the soul that the battleground exists.

> Abstain from fleshly lusts, which war against the
> soul. (1 Peter 2:11)

> For the good that I would I do not: But the evil
> which I would not, that I do. (Romans 7:19)

First the spirit of man is born again.

> Verily, verily, I say unto thee, Except a man be
> born of water and of the Spirit, he cannot enter
> into the kingdom of God. (John 3:5)

The flesh of man is either controlled by the soul, the carnal nature, or is controlled by the Spirit. Our soul must relinquish its will to be led by our spirit. Truth is hidden even to us unless God deals with us and shines His light into our dark places. Even as the light shines, we are many times unaware of the sin of our hearts and minds and must trust in His dealings and judgments of us. Trying to understand is many times a task we cannot comprehend, nor is it always revealed to us. But the end result is always the same, less of us and more of Jesus, bringing about that peace that all men search for.

> All men seek for thee. (Mark 1:37)

So just as the reigning Babylonian tribes were defeated by the Jews upon their reentry into the promised land, so can we as

Christians defeat the Babylonians in our lives. To do so, our souls must be regenerated.

> And be not conformed to this world: but be ye
> transformed by the renewing of your mind, that
> ye may prove what is that good, and acceptable,
> and perfect, will of God. (Romans 12:2)

Praise God, for His Word and its power are life to us, the believer.

Chapter 5

Soulish Freedom

Not all of the Hebrew children desired to reenter the promised land and receive their inheritance. They preferred the life they had built for themselves on the eastern banks of the Jordan River. Others, under Joshua's command, disobeyed the instructions in how to overcome and defeat their enemies. But some, in accordance with God's command, conquered and destroyed their enemies by force and took their inheritance. In the same way, all Christians will not be freed of soulish traits. Not all Christians desire to have such a walk with Jesus. Christians are as varied as the twelve Hebrew tribes. There are as many different types of Christians in growth and depth with Jesus Christ as there are sizes and shapes of flowers and trees. All are beloved by our heavenly Father but very different, receiving from His kingdom according to their individual response to discipleship.

Christians make different choices. One Christian may decide that the choice of freedom from soulish captivity is too much to pay and make a decision against God's perfect will for that life. For the overcoming life is not the simple Christian life nor the one that all will understand. Many, many Christians, like the Jews, wish to remain on the eastern side of the Jordan and compromise God's Word. The full power of God's truth, though available to every seeker, is not sought after, so the full truth remains hidden to so many. To be a sold-out disciple of Christ costs us everything. Discipleship costs us everything, yet even in this life, we are promised a thirty, sixty, or hundredfold return.

> And every one that hath forsaken houses, or brethren, or sisters, or father, or mother, or wife, or children, or lands, for my name's sake, shall receive a hundredfold, and shall inherit everlasting life. (Matthew 19:29)

And let it always be remembered, and dearly so, that our multiplied return inevitably is knowing Him.

Let it be emphasized that just because our Babylonian traits are recognized does not mean that our flesh is forever under the control of our spirit and that our soul now is placed in total submission to our spirit. Historically, remnants of the tribes were always found to be in the court of Israel, even during her zenith period. So it is with the Christian; regardless of his growth and maturing with the Lord, there are always remnants to be contended with and hidden sins yet to be brought to light.

As a Christian that which we feel freed of suddenly confronts us alive and well; old feelings are aroused. The Word of God comes to us to rescue us. But many times, we cannot apply it, for the battle is on, the flesh has reacted, and the soul remembers the experience of being wounded; self has been dealt a blow. The soul, instead of behaving regenerated, swims around in old thought patterns, deadly to the new nature but comfortable, like an old pair of shoes or old wine skins.

> Neither do men put new wine into old bottles: else the bottles break, and the wine runneth out, and the bottles perish: but they put new wine into new bottles, and both are preserved. (Matthew 9:17)

This is referring to the indwelling of the Holy Spirit. It also can refer to the fact that we must change our thought patterns within our souls in order to be obedient to our spirit. Those old ways of doing, saying, feeling, and reacting to circumstances that happen in our lives must be radically changed and placed under the blood of Jesus. The truth must supersede our feeling. It no longer matters what we feel or think, what matters is what the Word of God does say about any particular situation, for what the Word says is the final and absolute authority for our life. Our souls must be willing to forget past occurrence and concentrate on truth—the truth of God's Word. God's Word has provisions for every single human need in this world and the world to come. There is absolutely nothing that the Word of God cannot overcome. God desires us, His children, to be overcomers. He did not say it would be easy, but He most assuredly promised us overcoming victory. If there were no problems, there could be no overcoming. God is very interested in our reaction and behavior as maturing Christians. For our reactions to life's problems are indicative of our maturity in Christ Jesus.

Our souls must succumb to our spirits. This conflict is very painful to the soul, for it does not want to relinquish its independence to the voice of the Spirit. This is the dying of self. In the midst of the battle of the mind, the soul is many times not even able to hear the Spirit due to the confusion caused by outward circumstances and reaction to old habits of behavior. It is here that reaffirmation of our determination to follow Jesus Christ at all cost is so important. Jesus has never left us, though we may find ourselves in a state of confusion. It is the acquiescing of our will to stand not on our own thoughts but to believe the Word of God, regardless of the soul's reaction and especially our feelings.

The believer experiences great suffering from time to time. For it must be remembered that, at this time, God is dealing with a soul that yearns for regeneration, but as yet, in this particular area or circumstance has not experienced it. To be captured by self-interest, self-love and self protection with no apparent end in sight is very painful. We hurt so greatly, part of us knowing surely it will pass. It is sin that the soul is suffering from, and the release is release from ourselves. But even when this knowledge is revealed, captivity is excruciating. These inward dealings are difficult to express but no less real and must be contended with by the believer who desires Jesus above all else.

This conflict occurs from time to time…it is the process of dying to self. The believer throws himself again on the cross and prays for God to work out what He deems necessary in our life. Repentance follows. In the midst of dying, it is difficult to see resurrection. But we are promised resurrection by the Lord Jesus. As we die, He resurrects. The resurrection of His life in ours is the fulfillment of all we wish to be and all we ever need. But just as resurrection is real, so is the death. Yet as painful as the death is, so the more glorious the resurrection is.

In the book of Matthew, we are told that the kingdom of God must be taken by force.

> And from the days of John the Baptist until now,
> the kingdom of heaven suffereth violence, and
> the violent take it by force. (Matthew 11:12)

This appears to be a paradox since every believer is well aware of the Gospel of Christ and His words of peace. Yet the Jews fought for their inheritance as they reentered the promised land. Observe the parallel for the Christian in the Spirit. The Hebrews returned to the promised land and conquered their inheritance. Fertile fields, livable homes, cared-for livestock, and prosperous cities awaited their arrival. God certainly poured out His blessings as His children conquered what was theirs to begin with. So it is with the Christian; we are to inhabit and occupy. The fat of the land is ours, yet Satan is there every step of the way to thwart our plans, weaken our faith, and attempt to kill, steal, and destroy what is ours by right of being children of the King.

In the Spirit, force here is the antithesis of what the natural man would do. Christians are required to live by faith and not be deterred by what is seen in the natural. The world will bring every obstacle possible into the path of the believer to attempt to destroy his faith. For example, the believer may be placed in a position where his finances are destroyed. The Word of God very plainly explains

God's principle of economics. If followed, prosperity inevitably follows, for the kingdom principle of sowing and reaping is in effect. God is in no hurry, and many times as believers, we either get ahead of God's plan, or we linger slowly behind. In either case, our refuge and strength are always the same—Jesus Christ. By taking the kingdom by force, which is standing on faith regardless of the apparent circumstances, we are made into the image of Jesus Christ, and fruit of the Spirit is multiplied in the life of the Christian, this being God's ultimate purpose in our lives.

But before any of this can take place, man must first decide to be a disciple of Jesus Christ. The born-again understands (our sin nature) Egypt and the necessity of leaving it. For growth is only available to those who dare ask God to reveal Himself. He reveals His perfection through our imperfections, His strengths through our weaknesses, and His power through our lack of power. We must first know Jesus in power. Then and only then can we comprehend that everything we do is because of Him. It is God who pulls us out of Egypt and then has us overcome the soulish traits of Babylonia, those things that beset our souls, in order to free us from ourselves.

Our responsibility then is obedience to the call of the Holy Spirit and relinquishment of our self-will to do the will of our Father. His call on our lives is just that, a call. Each call is different for each person yet the same walk, the same cross, the same denying of self. But each person is unique in his role, his gift, and his place within the body of Christ—no more striving, no more competition, no more petty jealousies, no more judgments of others. How does one reach such a goal? The obedience to the Holy Spirit will enable the believer to walk in the Spirit and do what is impossible in the flesh. And though we desire to walk in the Spirit, there is that inward battle against our flesh and the putting down of the strongholds of our souls. We must give ourselves totally to the Lord Jesus Christ. This is a lifetime commitment, a lifetime of a continuous learning experience.

Being born again and forgiven for our sins, the Lord calls us saints and we are cleansed before our heavenly Father by the wonderful power of the blood of Jesus Christ.

My little children, these things write I unto you,
that ye sin not. And if any man sin, we have an
advocate with the Father, Jesus Christ the righteous: And he is the propitiation for our sins:
and not for ours only, but also for the sins of the
whole world. (1 John 2:1–2)

Satan despises purity, for there is nothing pure in him. As sinners by nature, we are in his camp to begin with. Consequently, to
lose us to the walk of repentance is vile to Satan. Pride is his virtue.
Multitudes of Christians are not involved in the penitent life of putting down oneself almost moment by moment. The Christian over-
flowing with Jesus Christ and yielding continuously to the voice of
the Holy Spirit (which produces a humble, penitent, and hungering
heart after God) is abhorrent to Satan above all else. For this saint is
the apple of the Father's eye. Never being perfect but being perfectly
willing to confess his sin gives God a free reign to continually bring
this child into God's righteousness.

We find ourselves in captivity from time to time in order to
grow. Satan comes after us in every conceivable way. The Bible
teaches us that we must become aware of his wiles and tricks and lies.

Put on the whole armor of God, that ye may
be able to stand against the wiles of the devil.
(Ephesians 6:11)

As we look at some of the different tribes to be overcome, we
will then compare them to our soulish traits. For the desire of the
Holy Spirit is to bring things to light. The prince of darkness would
prefer to keep all things hidden. Man is made to feel that he alone has
experienced particular soulish captivity. Many times, his trek to freedom ends. But as the Bible says, all temptation is common to man.

There hath no temptation (trial) taken you but
such as is common to men: but God is faithful,
who will not suffer you to be tempted above that

ye are able; but will with the temptation also
make a way to escape, that ye may be able to bear
it. (1 Corinthians 10:13)

Satan wishes to isolate us, making us feel weird and strange, whereas God is building a body, not estranged at all but perfectly fitting with all parts equally important. How we, as believers, need to remember this!

Chapter 6

The Canaanites

We now turn our attention to look at some of the people who inhabited the promised land at this time.

> And Joshua said, Hereby ye shall know that the living God is among you, and that he will without fail drive out from before you the Canaanites, and the Hittites, and the Hivites, and the Perizzites, and the Girgashites, and the Amorites, and the Jebusites. (Joshua 3:10)

These seven different tribes will be discussed as there is a parallel for us to see in their physical life in comparison with our spiritual life.

Notice, interestingly enough, that God told Joshua in Joshua 3:10 that He would expel and destroy seven tribes within the promised land. There were however more than seven different groups of people living in this area. The number seven in the Bible means completeness and perfection. God rested on the seventh day.

> And on the seventh day God ended his work which he had made; and he rested the seventh day from all his work which he had made. And God blessed the seventh day and sanctified it:

because that in it he had rested from all his work
which God created and made. (Genesis 2:2–3)

Seven here is for completeness and finishing. Noah took the clean beasts into the ark by sevens.

Of every clean beast thou shalt take to thee by
sevens, the male and his female: and of beasts
that are not clean by two, the male and female.
(Genesis 7:2)

Notice the unclean beasts were taken in by twos.
Two is the biblical number for division. Within our souls, we have an either/or situation: We either serve Satan or we serve God.

No servant can serve two masters: for either he
will hate the one, and love the other; or else he
will hold to the one, and despise the other, Ye
cannot serve God and mammon. (Luke 16:13)

But it is the sevens that we are to understand here. For if God completes all, and seven is spiritual perfection then the unclean and division of two can be overcome by the blood of Jesus. In other words, though division certainly invades our lives, we can overcome our problems by the power of Jesus Christ in our lives. God promised to destroy the seven tribes of people in Joshua 3:10. We have the same promise in the spirit from God that, through the power and blood of Jesus Christ, we can overcome the soulish havoc in our minds and make our thoughts captive to the Word of God.

Where he saith, When he ascended up on high,
he led captivity captive and gave gifts unto men.
(Ephesians 4:2)

The Israelites enter Canaan land, which came to mean the entire area of Palestine. But there were also a people referred to as

Canaanites that were a part of the area that God had given to His chosen children. This is the first of the seven tribes that the Jews encountered in order to reenter and recapture their promised land.

> For all the land which thou seest, to thee will I
> give it, and to thy seed forever. (Genesis 13:15)

> Every place that the sole of your foot shall tread
> upon, that have I given unto you, as I said unto
> Moses. (Joshua 1:3)

God had spoken that it was theirs, but it still had to be taken by force on the faith that God would do as He said He would.

It is the same with Christians. We must take what is rightfully ours from the prince of this world by force, walking in the power of the Lord Jesus Christ.

> And from the days of John the Baptist until now
> the kingdom of heaven suffereth violence, and
> the violent take it by force. (Matthew 11:12)

We must fight the world for that which is ours by inheritance. Whereas the Israelites fought with natural weapons, our weapons are not carnal but spiritual.

> For though we walk in the flesh, we do not war
> after the flesh: (For the weapons of our warfare
> are not carnal, but mighty through God to the
> pulling down of strongholds). (2 Corinthians
> 10:3–4)

Our battle will definitely be upstream, against the tide of the world as the world attempts continuously to pull us back. Just as Joshua, by God's Word, defeated the Canaanites, we too defeat the Canaanites in our lives and souls by God's eternal Word.

Israel's first encounter was against Jericho, a Canaanite city.

> And it came to pass on the seventh day, that they rose early about the dawning of the day, and compassed the city after the same manner seven time: only on that day they compassed the city seven times. And it came to pass on the seventh time, when the priests blew with the trumpets, Joshua said unto the people, Shout; for the Lord hath given you the city. So the people shouted when the priests blew with the trumpets: and it came to pass, when the people heard the sound of the trumpet, and the people shouted with a great shout, that the wall fell down flat, so that the people went up into the city, every man straight before, and they took the city. (Joshua 6:15–16, 20) Jericho literally fell down.

The Canaanites were defeated as Israel took over one battle at a time. We too defeat our Canaanites a battle at a time. Our inner man replaces our soulish behavior with the indwelling presence of the Holy Spirit one step at a time. We become cleansed gradually.

> When the unclean spirit is gone out of a man, he walketh through dry places, seeking rest, and findeth none. Then he saith, I will return into my house from whence I came out; and when he is come, he findeth it empty, swept, and garnished. Then goeth he, and taketh with himself seven other spirits more wicked than himself, and they enter in and dwell there: and the last state of that man is worse than the first. Even so shall it be also unto this wicked generation. (Matthew 12:43–45)

We must submit self with the abundance of Christ Jesus and the Word of God, or we will find ourselves in a worse condition. This process involves time, experience, teaching, and an openness of our wills. It does not take place immediately, because the natural man fights this process…then this process is relinquishment of pride and dying to self. And there is a part of us that finds this abhorrent.

The Canaanites were descendants of Ham. The Canaanites were traders, in the business of selling sheep's wool. They produced crimson wool. The purple dye used was gotten from a sea mollusk, and the art of dyeing wool became a very lucrative business for the Canaanites. At this time, colors were not in popular usage. The upper classes immediately began to wear the crimson wool. It was a very short period of time before the color purple denoted opulence and aristocracy. The royalty of Egypt wore purple. During the Roman era, Roman senators wore purple tunics to indicate governmental status. Even through the Middle Ages, the Catholic Church used purple as ecclesiastical trappings. This is still true in many denominational churches today. (The color purple denotes worldliness in the Bible royalty, authority, kingship)

As an analogy, we find ourselves following Jesus dressed in spiritual purple or spiritual pride. Such is the world's cure for the zealous Christian. I he cannot be lured away, fill his life with good works, clothed in outer purple apparel. If the Christian insists on being in God's work then keep him busy. This person sweats through his Christian life, filling his life with hay and stubble.

> For other foundation can no man lay than that is laid, which is Jesus Christ. Now if any man build upon this foundation gold, silver, precious stones, wood, hay, stubble; Every man's work shall be made manifest: for the day shall declare it because it shall be revealed by fire; and the fire shall try every man's work of what sort it is. (1 Corinthians 3:11–13)

Our works for Jesus in the spirit are effortless. We literally float through our particular task. And regardless of the problems we may encounter, we are determined to complete the job, and the effort to do so is the Lord's. We are merely obedient servants, not so with the

Canaanite Christian. His wool clothing caused great sweat, and this Christian literally wore himself out.

Most persons in this category leave the church with memories of spaghetti dinners, Sunday school picnics, bridge benefits, bazaars, and a host of other events but no Jesus, no feeding of the spirit or soul. The outer garment has its devastating effect. It sweats out the believer.

Oh, what a magnificent God we serve. There is yet so much for Him to teach us. We learn, "He hath made every thing beautiful in his time: also he hath set the world in their heart, so that no man can find out the work that God maketh from the beginning to the end" (Ecclesiastes 3:11). Our God is fully aware of the necessity of enabling us to shed our purple woolen garments in order to serve Him through the spirit.

> Even so faith, if it hath not works, is dead, being
> alone. (James 2:17)

There are of course "works" that must be done as we follow Jesus Christ. But rather than acting on our initiative, we must wait on the leading of the Lord. Then rather than sweating through our task and complaining bitterly, perhaps only inwardly, we realize that any obstacles met are not against us but against the Word that resides within us. For persecution cometh because of the Word. It is Satan against God. It is only when God has commanded us to complete a task that, through His strength, we are able to carry it out with the grace that is pleasing to our Father. In this way, we shed the wool of the Canaanites and replace our garment with linen, a material that enables the flow of the Holy Spirit to move undisturbed. We cease to do those things that the world most assuredly would notice and give us credit for. We remove our purple wool and replace it with His works done in secret, known only to our heavenly Father who rewards.

> And they drove not out the Canaanites that
> dwelt in Gezer: but the Canaanites dwell among

the Ephraimites unto this day, and serve under
tribute. (Joshua 16:10)

Realize that, in spite of all our efforts, we are not totally free
from the pull of the world. For all our undressing of purple and all
our desire to shed wool for linen, we can still be snared by the world
from time to time. Innately, we are sinners. The world system is our
home; it is there that our flesh and unregenerated soul feel comfortable. Our flesh man spends all of his efforts and time protecting his
ego. He hides himself in purple and makes himself look good doing
"good works" even while he sweats. To allow the Spirit of God total
freedom and reign is the antithesis of the natural man. It is a day-
to-day overcoming to place the Canaanites under the dominion of
our spirit. Definitely, our choice is not made one time only. The
Canaanites nip at our heels continuously. Praise God for repentance
as we fall and are snared over and over again by those things we
thought we were totally free of.

Both the Egyptians and the Canaanites are types of the world
system. Though representing the same outward story of the world's
snare against us, the inward story, though it may appear the same, is
quite different in regard to our makeup. In Egypt, we are living in the
world system. We are in bondage to it. Just as the Hebrew children
were slaves to the Egyptians, we too, while in the world, are slaves to it.
Remember that man is not aware of the chains and shackles upon him,
for it is all he has ever known. Only as God frees us are we aware of
our bondage. Thus our flesh is in slavery in Egypt to the world system.
God calls us to come out of the world. He exhorts us and prays for His
children in chapter 17 of John that we be in the world but not of the
world. The Hebrew children are freed from Egypt and are now seizing
the promised land to find again the world system in the Canaanites.

However, whereas in Egypt, we discover our flesh and its wickedness. It is in the seizing of Canaan that we begin our soul battle.
There is great significance here. Without soul regeneration, the flesh,
though freed from Egypt and removed, always yearns to return. If
the soul itself is not regenerated and filled with Jesus, the flesh will
always return to Egypt, for flesh is of this world. God removes us

from Egypt. He calls us out and delivers us from the bondage of the world and its system. However, in Canaan, it is our responsibility to take over and seize Canaan land by force. Though most assuredly, God is with us, and without His power of the Holy Spirit, such would be impossible. It is now our responsibility to will ourselves to overcome and destroy Canaan in our minds. We must continuously fill our minds and souls with the Word of God and the willingness of our inner man to obey the Spirit of God, regardless of the apparent cost at that immediate time. We shall not receive freedom or deliverance until we first stand.

It is always by pressing inward and closer to God through faith that we come into freedom. How few ever find it. And just as the Hebrew did not totally destroy the Canaanites, even yet we are unable and unwilling to destroy those areas in our soul. It is the thought processes, imaginations, and memories that snare us many times. We drift back into the world, for it is comfortable. Our flesh and soul have their original habitat in the world.

Just as many of the Jews pressed into the promised land, there are Christians who press on and on. Aware of the lingering Canaanites and knowing that, periodically, sin and failure are inevitable for the believer, he nevertheless presses ever onward to inhabit the entire land given to Him by God. It is a glorious story. Always our failure is His victory. The more we fall and realize that, in ourselves, we are capable of nothing, the closer we become to the heart of God. While He does require us to mature and desire for us to take what is ours by force, at the same time, we become more dependent on Him who is our strength and redeemer.

We fill our minds and souls with unceasing prayer and thoughts of Jesus who is life. We place our imaginations under the blood of Christ. We have left Egypt. Now in the promised land, though Canaanites are present, God, by the power of His Holy Spirit, quickens our hearts as to what we should do, and then obedience is up to us. But without knowing Him and His Word, we cannot be obedient to the voice. We do not even hear it or want to hear it. But for those who again have chosen Jesus Christ above all else, the voice is heard and the path lighted by Him one step at a time.

Chapter 7

The Hittites

The Hittites were another group of people who had settled in Canaan land. They mainly struggled to control the trade routes. They were a warlike people and secular historians give the Hittites credit for first using the metal, iron ore. The use of iron by the Hittites made them a powerful army as their weapons took on a new dimension of invulnerability, and with the other inhabitants of the promised land, they joined forces to fight against the Jews. The Hittites were defeated by the Jews, and years later, some Hittite women were found captive in Solomon's harem.

> And to the Canaanite on the east and on the west, and to the Amorite, and the Hittite, and the Perizzite, and the Jebusite in the mountains, and to the Hivite under Hermon in the land of Mizpeh. And they went out, they and all their hosts with them, much people, even as the sand that is upon the seashore in multitude, with horses and chariots very many. And when all these kings were met together, they came and pitched together at the waters of Merom, to fight against Israel. And the Lord said unto Joshua, Be not afraid because of them: for tomorrow about this time will I deliver them up all slain before

Israel: thou shalt hough their horses, and burn their chariots with fire. So Joshua came, and all the people of war with him, against them by the waters of Merom suddenly; and they fell upon them. And the Lord delivered them into the hand of Israel, who smote them, and chased them unto great Zidon, and unto Misrephothamanim, and unto the valley of Mizpeh eastward; and they smote them, until they left them none remaining. And Joshua did unto them as the Lord bade him: he houghed their horses, and burnt their chariots with fire. (Joshua 11:3–9)

Joshua obeyed the Lord God, and his enemy was defeated and placed into his hands. As we read on into chapter 11 of Joshua, we find the children of Israel inherited cities, cattle, plowed fertile fields, homes, etc. sitting ready for the children of Abraham to possess. The blessings of God flowed upon His children. Others did the work, and the Israelites inherited, for they obeyed God explicitly in the matter of battling these people. The will of the Jews bent totally to the will and command of God. Obedience brought the blessings of God.

The Hittites are a type for us to look at in regard to their use of iron ore. We can compare their physical use of iron to our spiritual iron wills. Many years later, the discovery and use of iron brought the industrial age into being and changed the course of mankind. But the real miracle of iron ore is the smelting of it into steel. Iron is hard but brittle. It is not flexible and does not stretch or contract with changes of weather. Iron cannot be worked with or molded into other forms easily, whereas steel possesses all the above properties. Steel is stronger than iron because it is flexible and will expand in the heat and contract in the cold without splitting or breaking. Steel can be made into thin strings of individual wire or bound together into strong cords of columns. It can be bent, twisted, curved, and worked any manner necessary to form it for the task it is meant for.

In the same way God wants a people who have wills not like iron but rather like steel. And God Himself is the alloy to our iron will that enables us to become like steel.

> Because I knew that thou art obstinate, and thy
> neck is an iron sinew, and thy brow brass. (Isaiah
> 48:4)

God desires to break our wills and bring them under the guidance of His will. Ultimately, our will must be broken and we become brother and sisters of Him who purchased us for a price.

> For ye are bought with a price: therefore glorify
> God in your body, and in your spirit, which are
> God's. (1 Corinthians 6:20)

As a member of family of the Lord Jesus Christ, demonic activity in our life is made captive, and we walk in freedom. For Jesus overcame the world, and He desires the same for us as he dwells within us in power, in truth, and in love. He, and He alone, knows what is best for us as He knows all things. Our decisions are limited, regardless of the amount of time and effort we put into our thoughts. Our wills are always subject to doing what we believe will help us. Our selfish motives are tied up in our wills and our desire to control. Our iron wills are destructive to us, having our own way is not the way to happiness or fulfillment in life.

When we demand our own way we generally find that we are the most unhappy of all creatures. The getting of our own way is an empty victory when we have imposed ourselves upon others. We not only want others to do things our way but to enjoy our way as well. Forcing our way and our will upon others, continuously crossing their will, does not bring us the peace we search for. Yet each time we are confronted with relinquishing our way for someone else, our iron will once again demands its own way. It is only in relinquishing our will to Jesus Christ that we can overcome the demand of self and bring ourselves into humbleness.

Look at the case of Solomon, a man of great wisdom who listened to his own flesh and turned from God. God endowed Solomon with great wisdom on the one hand but on the other hand warned him against the desires of his flesh, especially in regard to women. Many times in Scripture, the Word, woman refers to the flesh of man, while the word man refers to his spirit.

> Let the woman learn in silence with all subjection. But I suffer not a woman to teach, nor to usurp authority over the man, but to be in silence. (1 Timothy 2:11–12)

The church does not need to hear from "woman" or the flesh of man. The spiritual man is the one we wish to see rule.

> There is neither male nor female: for ye are all one in Christ Jesus. (Galatians 3:28)

We are all one in the Lord, male and female alike. And it is the inner man that is born again, filled with the Spirit, desiring to relinquish his will to the will of God. This does not mean to say that God does not have an order for male-female relationships. God has established a hierarchal line of authority for us. There is a church authority, a governmental authority, and a family authority we as Christians are commanded to obey with reverence.

Solomon brought foreign women into his harem, and they in turn began to practice their own occult religions. In a short period of time, Solomon too was worshipping other gods. The Hittite women within his harem were indicative of his iron will. Solomon heeded not the advice and counsel of God but obeyed his own desires and inclinations. Solomon, like so many of his modern counterparts, forgot from whom he received his wisdom and fell to his own fleshly desires. Flesh, is never improved, not even by wisdom. It is subject to outbursts at all times. Flesh must be placed always under the Spirit's direction. The presence of the Hittite women found later in Solomon's harem is a type for us as Christians. It is a reminder that we have our will, which can be in direct opposition to the will of God.

Solomon's reign was the height of Israel's national success and acclaim, and yet all their enemies had not been destroyed, evidenced of Hittite women in Solomon's harem. (The Hittites were subject to Israel's rule but were present nevertheless. The same is true with the believer today. Though as Christians, we may have matured with the Lord in that our desire is to relinquish our will to the will of the Father. The fact is, our own will is always present, hence the Hittite, and is subject to eruption.) Solomon's decision to choose his way over God's way, regardless of his wisdom, proved to destroy him. We too must be aware of our iron will and allow God to break it; to choose His way over our own. He alone truly knows our makeup what which would be best for our ultimate good. Therefore, we must seek God's will before we make a decision, or our will is in control and not subject to the will of God.

As Christians who love Jesus with all their hearts, we still allow ourselves to be duped so many times, especially by falling into the fallacy of believing we have given all to Jesus. Our prayers are sincere and from the heart, but when Jesus comes to collect on what we have so easily said we would relinquish, we find a battle of wills at hand. Suddenly we rear up inside, and our will is diametrically opposed to the Lord's. We feel, surely, He has made a mistake, and what He is asking for is not what we meant at all. We are pliable, manageable pieces of clay, until the Lord crosses our will. The Lord is chipping away at our wood or our carnal nature, desiring to mold it into His image, but our defiant will stands in His way. For many Christians, the carnal will can be hardened, and the process that God intends is slowed down and perhaps even halted for a time.

> So he went with them. And when they came to
> Jordan, they cut down wood. But as one was fell-
> ing a beam, the axe head fell into the water: and
> he cried, and said, Alas, master! for it was bor-
> rowed. And the man of God said, Where fell it?
> And he showed him the place, And he cut down

a stick, and cast it in thither; and the iron did swim. Therefore said he, Take it up to thee, And he put out his hand, and took it. (2 Kings 6:4–7)

As the Father is molding us into His image, cutting down the wood, we allow our will to submit to His. The axe head, our will over the Father falls into the water. The water is the Word of God. As we allow His Word to work in us we find that our will floats in the water. Our iron will is made so pliable that it does the unnatural thing by floating on the water. We do the opposite of the carnal man.

We relinquish all of our rights to the Father, determined to do that which He would have us to do. And the beauty here is the floating of our will. For this brittle hard axe head floats on the water, and we can pick it up with our hand. What we generally stand so firm against, we find that when we give it to the Father, He returns it to us. But the bondage is broken; the iron is pliable, floating in the Word of God. Once again, whatever it was that owned us and demanded that part of us that God felt it necessary to rid from our life is now gone and put under the authority of Jesus Christ.

Many times, our emotions are involved with our iron will. Our love for objects, people, or places has superseded our love for the Father. We are determined to keep our idol. Our mind is set upon a particular path, and we refuse to change. Suddenly our will is in conflict with God's. He calls us to change. We resist. It always goes back to self, a love of self, and our way over the Lord's. We come not only into conflict with the Father's desire for us but conflict in our emotions as well. We don't feel like doing what He has called us to do. Many times, we falter and resist because of our feelings. We allow our feelings to override our judgment. Once again, the dying of self is a continuous process. We seek His will. We relinquish our will. Our sin has been revealed to us by the Holy Spirit. We must now deal with the sin. We can no longer ignore it. How quickly we relinquish ourselves to the Spirit of God determines how quickly we can move out of the bondage that sin has held us in.

Jesus answered them, Verily, verily, I say unto you, Whosoever committeth sin is the servant of sin. (John 8:34)

Know ye not, that to whom ye yield yourselves servants to obey, his servants ye are to whom ye obey; whether of sin unto death, or of obedience unto righteousness? (Romans 6:16)

Being then made free from sin, ye became the servants of righteousness. (Romans 6:18)

Whenever we attempt to hang onto something, refusing to let go of it by giving it to the Father, we are merely keeping ourselves in bondage to something that God desires to free us from. Jesus came that we might be set free in this life, in this world. Any time He asks for something of our life it is always because He knows we shall be better off without it. He desires for us to walk in freedom, to have all things under our feet as they are under His feet. It is the same thing that Jesus spoke to Paul, "It is hard for thee to kick against the pricks." Whatever we are holding onto, give it up to the Father. He alone can free us and enable us to have the abundant life that He desires for us to have. But we must relinquish our wills at His calling, His timing, His demand. We must be obedient. He is God; we are man. He is the potter; we are the clay Isaiah 64:8.

We come into conflict with God every day with every decision we make. For always, the question is, His way or our way? Our stubborn will, is made pliable by Jesus, and we give our way to His way. We exchange bondage for freedom. This life as a Christian is one of faith, believing and accepting the Lord will do as He has spoken. We cannot have the healing until we experience the victory by faith. We must stand on faith then in the flesh, as time passes, the healing will manifest itself, whether it is physical or emotional. The time period from victory by faith to healing is that time where we have done all and now must stand and see the salvation of our God.

> Wherefore take unto you the whole armor of
> God, that ye may be able to withstand in the evil
> day, and having done all, to stand. (Ephesians
> 6:13)

In the dream of Nebuchadnezzar, the prophet Daniel is given by God the interpretation of the dream that pertains to the end-times. The great image seen by the king is representative of the past, present, and future kingdoms on earth. All this must take place before the second coming of Jesus Christ. This prophecy is given six hundred years before the birth of Jesus Christ!

> His legs of iron, his feet part of iron and part
> of clay. Thou sawest till that a stone was cut out
> without hands, which smote the image upon his
> feet that were of iron and clay, and brake them
> to pieces…and the stone that smote the image
> became a great mountain, and filled the whole
> earth. (Daniel 2:33–35)

This particular passage of Scripture is referring to the Roman empire and to the birth of Jesus Christ. The Hittite in man is his iron will, our will over God's will. The rebellion that resides in man could never be overcome without Jesus Christ. Even the law given by God to teach man righteousness could not break or annul man's iron will and rebellion against God.

> For what the law could not do, in that it was
> weak through the flesh, God sending his own
> Son in the likeness of sinful flesh, and for sin,
> condemned sin in the flesh. (Romans 8:3)

In Daniel 2:34, we see that the stone was cut without hands (Jesus Christ) and smote the image of iron (Man and his iron will). In verse 35, the stone, Jesus Christ, filled the whole earth. The presence of the Holy Spirit is now upon the earth; and once and for all, the spirit of rebellion of Satan is forever broken for those who choose Jesus and forsake the world and its system. Christians overcome rebellion by the power of Jesus Christ in their lives. The Holy Spirit, like the great mountain in verse 35, fills the earth and frees mankind from his curse! What the law could not do, Jesus does. Man, doomed forever under his own yoke of rebellion, pushed by his own iron will, is now free, and the yoke has been broken forever.

As we approach the throne room of our heavenly Father, we can but praise God for His freeing us of our Hittite heritage. Only as we bend our wills to God's will will we ever be complete. There is no happiness for us as His creation outside of His perfect will for our lives. And there is no abiding in His will until we lay down our will. We then, as the great stone, or Jesus, become the lively stones.

> To whom coming, as unto a living stone, disallowed indeed of men, but chosen of God, and precious, Ye also, as lively stones, are built up a spiritual house, a holy priesthood, to offer up spiritual sacrifices, acceptable to God by Jesus Christ. (1 Peter 2:4–5)

Our iron will is a root of our sinful nature. As Christians, it is a daily battle and a daily commitment to lay our wills at the feet of our Father and relinquish our way to His way. We follow Him but through faith, not always understanding His way and His will for our lives but walking in that obedience because we know Him and know that He truly is God, our Creator. We shall fall short of this victory many times. We are thankful for the cleansing blood of Jesus Christ; oh, how we need Him!

Chapter 8

The Hivites

And the men of Israel said unto the Hivites,
Peradventure ye dwell among us; and how shall
we make a league with you?

—Joshua 9:7

The Hivites are mentioned in the Old Testament sixteen times and always in connection to Israel. There has been no known recorded historical data found on the Hivites. And outside of biblical history, little, if anything, is known about these people. Chapter 9 in Joshua gives us a very interesting story about the Hivites and their character. They were ingenious as deceivers!

The Hivites of Gibeon, along with all the neighboring tribes in the Canaan area, were well aware of the Jewish exploits and their recent victories over the city of Jericho and Ai. A fear of the Israelites had spread throughout the land, for the people had all heard of these Hebrews and their powerful God. God had instructed the Israelites not to make peace with any of the inhabitants of the promised land but to destroy everything and take the land, which He had preordained for them. The Hivites, fully aware of this, came up with a plan with which to deceive the Jews and thereby save their city from destruction. The Hivites convinced the Israelites that they were people from a distant land who wished to live in peace with the Israelites.

Dressed in torn, ragged clothes, and carrying decayed food and old provisions, it appeared that the Hivites had traveled from afar. The Israelites were duped, and a league of peace was made with these people. When the truth of the Hivites was discovered by the Israelites, the Jews, faithful to their word and peace treaty, did not kill the Hivites but cursed them to be hewers of wood and drawers of water for the house of God. The Christian can see himself in this situation, both as the deceived Jew and the deceivers themselves, the Hivites.

How quickly we forget the mighty, powerful hand of God. We think we need the spectacular to mightily believe, but miracles are soon forgotten. In reality, our need is more and more of Jesus, pressing into Him for who He is, not what He gives. Knowing Him for who He is, we always receive what He has for us. It is a faith walk and that in itself is spectacular. It is not a walk of miraculous events or mountaintop experiences. Constant mountaintop experiences would prevent a walk of faith, for there are valleys in life that must be contended with too. If we had nothing but successes, we would move without seeking direction from the Holy Spirit, feeling God would surely take care of us if we made a wrong move. God is a Father, however not a Santa Claus. We must learn obedience and total dependence on Him. We must learn to seek His direction before we act.

God had called forth a people from the midst of Babylonia through one man. Abraham, through faith, became the friend of God. His descendants inherited the promised land, Canaan. Due to a famine, the Jews then went into Egypt where they were held in captivity for four hundred years as slaves. God miraculously freed the Hebrews, dramatically parted the Red Sea, and destroyed the enemy army. He cared for His children in the desert with shoes and clothes that never wore out, provided food upon the ground daily, and yet still disobedience rang out in the ranks. Upon re-entering the promised land, the commandment of God to destroy everything was disobeyed over and again.

The Jews consistently had problems with the different peoples that remained within their borders. These people lured the Israelites to go against the one and only God. Shortly, the worship of idols became part of the Israelite life. The Jews, because of disobedience, found themselves leavened. Eventually, compromise upon compromise brought about the destruction of the Hebrew nation, and she was split asunder.

> Every kingdom divided against itself is brought
> to desolation; and every city or house divided
> against itself shall not stand. (Matthew 12:25)

God will not allow us to mock His name. We shall not claim to be His and live and follow after other gods. Destruction is inevitable, for we will reap what we sow.

We so quickly judge the Israelite. How could anyone turn away from God after experiencing such miracles? Why would a people turn to idols when they had tasted and seen God's magnificent hand in their lives? But before we so quickly judge the Hebrew, we need only to look at our own lives and the life of our nation. The United States of America has been blessed above all nations in the world. Our wealth and prosperity cannot even be compared to any other country. Our lives have been filled with freedoms and blessings preserved by God. This nation founded on His principles and rooted deeply in His Word is now ridiculing the very Father who made it all possible.

And like the Jews, as God has showered His blessings and miracles upon us, we have gone whoring after other gods. We too began our trek downward as we compromised on God's Word and began to do those things that looked good to us, rather than those things God commanded us to do. We began to give credit to ourselves for all our multitudes of successes and refused to seek the counsel of God or obey His eternal principles. We believed our thoughts superseded His and that we knew better than God.

> For my thoughts are not your thoughts, neither
> are your ways my ways, saith the Lord. For as the
> heavens are higher than the earth, so are my ways
> higher than your ways, and my thoughts than
> your thoughts. (Isaiah 55:8–9)

We have allowed sin to be excused rather than judged. Now the very fibers of our nation seem to be stretched to the limit and only intervention by our Father will save us from destruction.

Just as Israel is made up of Israelites, so is the United States made up of Americans. So it is not nations that turn from Jesus Christ; it is people. It is us. We must deny ourselves and return to following God's laws. As we repent as individual people, God will sovereignly move in behalf of the United States, and where we deserve wrath, we will receive mercy.

> If my people, which are called by my name, shall
> humble themselves, and pray, and seek my face,
> and turn from their wicked ways; then will I hear
> from heaven, and will forgive their sin, and will
> heal their land. (2 Chronicles 7:14)

We are not called to criticize everything around us, finding fault with the system and laws that confront us. We are called to obey Christ and spread His Gospel. As this is done, repentance will take place, and people will not just be touched but changed.

Some will obviously do more than others, "for many be called, but few chosen" (Matthew 20:16). We need only to study the beatitudes in chapters 5, 6, and 7 in the book of Matthew to see how God truly requires and expects more from His own. It is our call into the world. It is how we truly shine our light from Him and do not put our candle under a bushel. We are called to be servants, not to be served. We are to be the salt of the earth, doing more than is required and always with a willing heart, not a pious, self-righteous good work attitude.

> Ye are the light of the world. A city that is set on a
> hill cannot be hid. Neither do men light a candle,
> and put it under a bushel, but on a candlestick;
> and it giveth light unto all that are in the house.
> Let your light so shine before men, that they may

see your good works, and glorify your Father
which is in heaven. (Matthew 5:14–16)

Not all Christians are interested in such a walk with God. But
for those who choose to press onward into Canaan, it is the only
walk. As the Holy Spirit reveals more of ourselves to us, we die, and
He lives through us.

There are always times when those that should, do not do as
they should. But the Christian is there to take up the slack to do
more than is necessary, go the extra mile.

And whosoever shall compel thee to go a mile, go
with him twain. (Matthew 5:41)

For truly, it rains on the saved and unsaved, and God blesses all
for the efforts of His chosen few.

That ye may be the children of your Father which
is in heaven: for he maketh his sun to rise on the
evil and on the good, and sendeth rain on the just
and on the unjust. (Matthew 5:45)

And as we, pray for our nation and do we are called to do, we
can keep men of God in public office. We shall place godly laws upon
our books. Morality will again prevail in our society, and, God willing, our schools will perpetuate our way of life and cease to be zoos
and institutions of corruption. But the change must first take place
in the home, in the life of the individual.

Both the Hivite and the Jew are a type for us as Christians.
The men of Gibeon did deceive Joshua and his elders. Everything
looked like the truth, but the counsel of God was not sought. Joshua
depended on what he saw instead of what was, for the Hivites
appeared to be what in reality they were not.

And the men took of their victuals, and asked not
counsel at the mouth of the Lord, And Joshua

made peace with them, and made a league with
them, to let them live: and the princes of the con-
gregation sware unto them. (Joshua 9:14–15)

How often Christians do exactly the same thing. We allow circumstances to sway us in our decision-making instead of following and depending on the Word of God. And, too, we do not seek God in prayer for making decisions as we should. Lack of communing with our Father allows leaven to creep into our lives and leaven influences us in our decision-making. We then make up our minds on what seems to be the logical thing to do at the time, or we get our eyes on the circumstances instead of obeying the Word of God to the letter.

God had instructed Joshua to destroy the tribes that inhabited the Promised Land. The Hivites could have been who they pretended to be, a people from a land afar. The sin of the Jew was that the counsel of God was not sought. Not seeking God's counsel caused the Israelites to then disobey God in regard to the treatment of the Hivites. If we disobey one of God's laws, we will find ourselves faltering in other areas, for His instructions are given and learned by us one step at a time.

But the word of the Lord was unto them precept
upon precept, precept upon precept; line upon
line, line upon line; here a little; and there a little; that they might go, and fall backward, and
be broken, and snared, and taken. (Isaiah 28:13)

So many times, we feel we can handle the situation that we can move forward on our own, that prayer is not necessary. We are being disobedient to the little things. God's desire for our lives is for us to seek Him in everything. As events appear to fall into place, we assume that God has ordained our direction, and we move ahead rather cockily and in our own strength, not depending on our Father and His explicit instructions. This is our sin, once again attempting to do things our way. It is innate sin to believe we can accomplish things ourselves without total dependence on God. We are oblivious to the idea that anything but good would come out of our independent moves and decisions. Are we not the chosen ones of God? Indeed, but He will have obedience above sacrifice. We must train our minds to seek Him first. That is not the natural way, especially in the midst of our successes. In failures, we always seek God first. But in successes, we often tend to move too hastily or forget to seek counsel at all. We fail, but our failures take us back to God. We begin again at the point of seeking His counsel! What a marvelous God we serve. His arms always stretch out to take us back, regardless of our failures. His requirement is just that we admit we are wrong and that we need Him; and then our entire lives are changed back to His perfect direction from the mixed-up, mismanaged course of destruction we were headed on.

Joshua realized his error, repented and sentenced the Hivites to be drawers of water and hewers of wood.

> Now therefore ye are cursed, and there shall none
> of you be freed from being bondmen, and hewers
> of wood and drawers of water for the house of my
> God. (Joshua 9:23)

Joshua did not break his league of peace with the men of Gibeon and kill them as he would like to, for Jewish law prevented Joshua from being a covenant breaker.

> This we will do to them; we will even let them
> live, lest wrath be upon us, because of the oath
> which we sware unto them. (Joshua 9:20)

We cannot, as people, make wrong right. We must and will pay for the consequences of our mistakes. Had Joshua killed the Hivites at this time, he would have been trying to justify his disobedience in not obeying God in the first place.

> And so did he unto them, and delivered them
> out of the hand of the children of Israel, that they
> slew them not. (Joshua 9:26)

We attempt to make deals with God. But we do not right wrong. We are to be penitent for our sins and mistakes and then give them all to God, realizing and believing that He alone has the power to make all things work together for good. Our attempt to right our wrong is merely an attempt to hide our disobedience in the first place. Joshua was commanded to destroy every tribe he encountered. He did not do so with the Hivite, nor did he seek counsel of the Lord. In such human failures, we are always trying to justify our actions and make ourselves look good and right. We would do best to leave things in the hand of God, admitting our wrongdoing and then, in faith, believe and know that God is indeed in control. This Joshua did. After discovering how the Hivites had deceived him, he did not kill them, adding disobedience to disobedience.

As the deceived, we fall into sin. Are we also the deceivers as well? Indeed. The Hivites are a part of our soulish makeup. By nature, we are deceivers, trying always to appear to be what we are not in hopes of pleasing people and bringing gratification to self. Mankind is a great imposter hiding behind facades to create a false sense of security and well-being. Satan attempts to keep all things hidden.

> If we say that we have fellowship with him, and
> walk in darkness, we lie, and do not the truth:
> But if we walk in the light, as he is in the light, we
> have fellowship one with another, and the blood
> of Jesus Christ his Son cleanseth us from all sin.
> (1 John 1:6–7)

God reveals the truth and urges us to disrobe ourselves, thus disarming Satan. We must admit to being sinners, repent, and find freedom and power in the Lord Jesus Christ. Self must die. And though the ego recoils at this idea, the inner man thrives upon it as he grows ever stronger, bringing contentment and strength to the entire body.

> For which cause we faint not; but though our out-
> ward man perish, yet the inward man is renewed
> day by day. (2 Corinthians 4:16)

Our flesh always lies in order to exalt our ego. We naturally lie; only Jesus is the truth. His presence in us draws us into truth about ourselves and our relationship to others as we relinquish ourselves to Him.

The Hivites, whose true identity is discovered by the Jews, are then cursed to forever be hewers of wood and drawers of water in the house of God.

> Now therefore ye are cursed, and there shall none
> of you be freed from being bondmen, and hewers
> of wood and drawers of water for the house of my
> God. (Joshua 9:23)

The Hivites, though alive physically, are in bondage to the Israelites they had so greatly feared. We too can be very much alive physically but find ourselves in bondage. As Christians, who love the Lord, we are not so much in bondage to the world anymore. For we have long since left Egypt; but we are now dealing with our souls and overtaking Canaan, which is our inheritance. So bondage is deep-seated and even can appear good. Spiritually speaking, the Hivites within us are so well hidden that, without the light of the Holy Spirit, we would not even know that they were there.

Hewers of wood are those soulish traits of our own where we attempt to make ourselves be like Jesus. We force behavior upon ourselves that is not natural; we pretend even within ourselves. The hewer of wood, instead of allowing the Holy Spirit to chip away the wood or chaff to make us into the image of Jesus, does the work himself and then takes credit for it. A temper that has not flared in months has merely not had the correct pressure placed upon it. Yet we feel we are better and that the temper is gone. This simply is not true. Certainly, the irate temper that flared constantly is now under control. But to claim to have no temper is to deceive ourselves.

> If we say that we have no sin, we deceive our-
> selves, and the truth is not in us. (1 John 1:8)

We begin to pride ourselves inside on the fact that our temper has not flared up. Before long, we take credit for the working within us, not submitting to the Holy Spirit. When this takes place and our temper rises, we refuse to admit to it and thus move into deceit against ourselves. We constantly then try to hew or shape ourselves into Jesus's image instead of once again relinquishing our own wills, repenting when we fall so short and allowing the Spirit to work freely within us.

> If we confess our sins, he is faithful and just
> to forgive us our sins, and to cleanse us from
> all unrighteousness. If we say that we have not
> sinned, we make him a liar, and his word is not
> in us. (1 John 1:9–10)

A drawer of water is another soulish trait we must contend with. Here we find ourselves attempting to work up a spiritual experience for ourselves, to move always in a supernatural spiritual way. We forget that to occupy the earth most of the time means to go about our daily tasks with God in the midst of them. We are busy drawing upon spiritual water, or so we think, to accomplish works we were never called to do in the first place. We need to merely relinquish our wills to the Father, and He will bring us into those things He has called us to do.

The Hivites are not only difficult to recognize within ourselves, but also, it must be remembered that they generally appear to be good. It is just that, in reality, unless the Holy Spirit directs our actions, nothing is good. Goodness belongs to the Father. We, like the Hivites, must take our good to the altar.

> Why callest thou me good? There is none good
> but one, that is, God: but if thou wilt enter into
> life, keep the commandments. (Matthew 19:17)

> And Joshua made them that day hewers of wood
> and drawers of water for the congregation, and
> for the altar of the Lord, even unto this day, in
> the place which he should choose. (Joshua 9:27)

Without the conviction of the Holy Spirit, we could not even relinquish our "good" to God since there are many things we do that seem good to us and to those around us. If we are, for example, fasting and the Lord has not directed so, it is not good. We give where He tells us to give; we speak what He tells us to speak and so forth. Our life is to be lived for Him and in Him in perfect obedience. We must hear His voice and follow what He tells us to do. And many times, because we see darkly now, we will be listening and following by faith alone. But it is this faith that is pleasing to our Father.

The Hivites are mentioned sixteen times in the Old Testament and always in connection with other tribes. Sixteen is the number for love. God's definition of love is given to us in sixteen different ways in 1 Corinthians chapter 13. It is God's perfection that He will most assuredly rid us of our hidden sins, our hidden thoughts of goodness about ourselves that inadvertently put us above Him, for such traits have been placed upon the cross. By the illuminating light of the Holy Spirit, we see our particular sin. The Holy Spirit shines into our darkness. We must then deal with the deceitfulness that has been brought to light. Our deceptions have been hidden for so long within us. For example, we are unable to see deep-rooted jealousy in our personalities until revealed to us by the Holy Spirit. Our own emotions deceive us so that we may think our jealousy is an expression of deep love or caring. Jealousy is a large part of the makeup of the carnal heart and so tied to self. It takes the Holy Spirit to define it for us, and even then, we relinquish our Hivite only slowly as it seems to be part of ourselves, and there is a part of us that does not even wish to be free. If the jealousy is thought to be love and must be relinquished, what happens to our love? Our lack of understanding God's love and our own emotions confuses us. We must again throw ourselves upon the cross. God is love, not what we have heard and been taught is love. He will bring about His love within us and complete us by His love. We need not fear, as the Holy Spirit is able and willing.

> Being confident of this very thing, that he which
> hath begun a good work in you will perform it
> until the day of Jesus Christ. (Philippians 1:6)

As it was with Satan, so it is with us. Our deepest sin is love of self, and everything that happens to us is related to our deep love of self. Our internal Hivite is love of self, and dying to ourselves is God's replacement of His love for our self-love. Our greatest freedom lies in forgetting ourselves and placing our entire emphasis on Jesus Christ. Our entire thrust in life as Christians is to continually enhance our vertical relationship, preferring Him over ourselves. In doing this, our horizontal relationships automatically begin to fall into place, and we become reconciled to the ministry we have been called to as Christians. We are then the ambassadors to the world Christ has called us to be. But this is only possible as we allow Him to work through us and die daily to self.

> And all things are of God, who hath reconciled
> us to himself by Jesus Christ, and hath given to
> us the ministry of reconciliation; To wit, that
> God was in Christ, reconciling the world unto
> himself, not imputing their trespasses unto them;
> and hath committed unto us the word of rec-
> onciliation. Now then we are ambassadors for
> Christ, as though God did beseech you by us:
> we pray you in Christ's stead, be ye reconciled to
> God. (2 Corinthians 5:18–20)

Little is known of the Hivites. The Bible does tell us what deceivers they are. And too, little is known by us of our love of self. We deceive ourselves. We are not aware of the love of self that captivates everything we do. Only the enlightenment of the Holy Spirit can reveal it to us. We need to relinquish ourselves to His teaching and guidance, and He will reveal us to ourselves, and our Hivite can be placed under the blood. Certainly, self does not die once and for all. And certainly, this is a daily process. Praise God for His everlasting love and patience.

Hivites are those hidden, unbeknownst sins. We sin, not knowing, but our wonderful Father forgives us and has us covered by the blood of Jesus Christ. We are covered for past present and future sins. He does all for us, and many times, we are not even aware!

Chapter 9

The Perizzites

As for all the people that were left of the
Hittites, and the Amorites, and the Perizzites,
and the Hivites, and the Jebusites, which
were not of Israel, but of their children, who
were left after them in the land, whom the
children of Israel consumed not, them did
Solomon make to pay tribute until this day.

—2 Chronicles 8:7–8

We see that the tribes are not totally destroyed but are under the rulership of Israel. The same is true for the believer. We do not become perfect or live a life totally void of sin, but we place ourselves under the rulership of the Holy Spirit.

The Perizzites are a people who are not totally destroyed and who come under the rulership of Israel at the time of Solomon. The Hittites and the Hivites have been discussed previously. It is easy to discern that our iron will is never obliterated but placed under obedience, as with the Hittites. The Hivites are those traits and sins that are hidden even to ourselves. They are under the blood of Jesus. The Perizzites were dwellers in unwalled villages in the open country of Palestine. They were a large population of people and inhabited the territory that was to belong to the tribe of Judah. In total, the Perizzites are mentioned in Scripture twenty-three times and are always found in lists of tens or fives with the other tribes.

These people too are a type of our soulish behavior. They inhabit Judah. Jerusalem then and now is in Judah. And Jerusalem is the geographical focal point in the world. It is God's choice of real estate. It is His city. When Jesus returns and resides in Jerusalem, the entire world will be under His perfect rule and will recognize Jerusalem as the center and place of royalty it is to be. The true beauty of God's choice will be seen outwardly. The rest of the world will be radiant because of Jerusalem, the focal point. It will be the presence of Jesus in Jerusalem that will fulfill her destiny. His presence is necessary for Jerusalem to become what God has spoken for her to be in Scripture. Jesus's presence in Jerusalem will give light and peace to the entire world. As the heart of the world is conquered and the proper King is reigning, the rest of the world will respond accordingly. Peace will reign.

There is a similarity here concerning man and his spirit. Jerusalem appears today to be yet in turmoil. By faith in the Word, we know what is yet to come to her. There is a parallel here in regard to the believer. The very essence of man, the central focal point is self. Self for the believer has been turned over to the Holy Spirit. But just as Jerusalem does not appear outwardly to be what she shall be, neither do we appear as we shall be. And just as Jerusalem needs Jesus to radiate and fulfill her destiny, so must we have Jesus to bring light into our darkened nature.

The Perizzites, though surrounding Jerusalem, do not themselves inhabit this particular area. The Jebusites inhabit Jerusalem. So before we can truly relinquish our self to God in the totality that He calls for, we must first conquer the outlying areas.

As was stated, the Perizzites are mentioned twenty-three times in the Old Testament and always in conjunction with other tribes in groups of fives and tens. The number twenty-three stands for death. There is a death of self that must be experienced in order for the believer to rid himself of the Perizzites. Ten is the number for law, and thirteen is the scriptural number for rebellion. Rebellion (thirteen) against the law (ten) causes death (twenty-three). So the

Perizzites, if never conquered and brought under the blood of Jesus Christ, bring us death. We are unable to inherit here in this life what the Lord has for us. Though eternally bound, we are earthly miserable. Perizzites, as people unwalled in ancient times, are symbolic of our mental thoughts going wild in vain imaginations, not being controlled by the Holy Spirit. We have the power by the Holy Spirit to put down our imaginations. Vain imaginations seem to always take us into thinking patterns that defeat rather than enhance our thinking.

> Casting down imaginations, and every high thought that cometh up against the knowledge of God, and bringing into captivity every thought to the obedience of Christ. (2 Corinthians 10:5)

Jesus describes rebellious man in Mark 7:20–23.

> And he said, That which cometh out of the man, that defileth the man. For from within, out of the heart of men, proceed evil thoughts, adulteries, fornications, murders, thefts, covetousness, wickedness, deceit, lasciviousness, an evil eye, blasphemy, pride, foolishness: All these evil things come from within, and defile the man.

This list of thirteen human traits describes man in his rebellious state. The Ten Commandments are the list of laws that state what man is commanded to do by God. However, righteousness did not come by the law but from the blood sacrifice of Jesus. And it is not we ourselves who are either able to obey the law or even desire to; it is the Holy Spirit who dwells within us who gives us the power to obey. It is the Holy Spirit who quickens our hearts to do what the law tells us to do, and it is God who then gives us the power to do so.

To rid ourselves of our Perizzites, we must listen to the voice of the Holy Spirit and take care not to grieve Him. In Romans 1:29–32, there is a list of twenty-three actions that grieve the Holy Spirit and cause death to us. So again, to take dominion over our Perizzites, we must be abiding in the Holy Spirit. We must continuously listen to His voice for instruction. It must be stressed that the believer (though always reaching for more of Jesus and always seeking Him) is never sin-free. By nature, we are sinners. Without the blood of Jesus, there would be no righteousness. Nevertheless, as we walk with the Lord and continue deep into our search of the character of Jesus, allowing that character to be made manifest in us, we taste life, victory, and peace in a capacity never experienced before. Repentance is a way of life. And instead of bemoaning the fact that we have sinned, we are readily willing to relinquish our pride and seek His forgiveness. We learn from our failing, He is always there when we fall so short. And though from time to time we do commit the same sins, there is a time when we have victory, and we do not so easily fall into the same old traps, which have always lured us. God patiently waits upon us for each victory and then takes us deeper into our inner man, for there is always another lesson for us. But with each lesson, there is ultimately a new victory, a new freedom, and a healing from within. All of this makes us overcomers. Jesus overcame the world by refusing to become a part of its system. He shared the Father's Word, the truth in a world of darkness. For everything in this world is built around the protection and exaltation of man's own ego. The truth enrages the pride of man.

Perizzites are dwellers in the open country. In order to hear the voice of the Holy Spirit, we cannot allow our minds to drift into the open country or be dwellers of thoughts of the world. We must keep a close watch upon the thoughts of our mind.

> No man that warreth entangleth himself with the
> affairs of this life; that he may please him who
> hath chosen him to be a soldier. (2 Timothy 2:4)

Television, movies, books, or other mental escapes are not evil in themselves but can cause the thought patterns to wander and bring in sin otherwise not dwelled upon. There is a balance in life. And though a monastic life is not advocated here, the mind must be fed. And as it is with the body, the mind will react to the food intake. Too much of the wrong thing will cause disease and chaos to the mind, which naturally causes sin. Once in a state of sin, the believer is not capable of hearing the Holy Spirit for the direction he needs, and peace and joy fade.

Consequently, things that once were acceptable are no longer so. As one moves closer into the center of God's will, his life changes; readjustments and denials take place. As the walk narrows, it becomes more difficult. And without the power and presence of the Holy Spirit, it is impossible to achieve with the Lord. Our thoughts must be diverted away from ourselves and toward the feelings and situation of others. We are forced to always seek to deny ourselves at the expense of our pride and humble ourselves before the Lord, bringing about a humility before our fellowman. Things we would once say, we no longer are permitted to say. Our tongues must be held, and we must remain in the background until God Himself deems it right or necessary for us to speak or make a move. How quickly we grieve the Holy Spirit. Only when He speaks are we to act. There is no justification for ourselves or our behavior. We are under the authority of the Holy Spirit and are to obey the voice of God. God will protect His reputation and the reputation of His vessel. God vindicates His own and brings vengeance against the wicked. We are called to obey His Word and His leadership. We are not permitted to fight the world on our own behalf to attempt to justify our thoughts and actions. We too are to be like sheep, dumb before our shearers.

> He was oppressed, and he was afflicted, yet he opened not his mouth: he is brought as a lamb to the slaughter, and as a sheep before her shearers is dumb, so he openeth not his mouth. (Isaiah 53:7)

The outer world, though it plagues the believer's mind, is not the battleground. It is the inward man in his mind that he must contend with. The battleground is wave upon wave of thoughts, rushing across the mind screen of man that are not of God at all.

> Let no man say when he is tempted, I am tempted
> of God: for God cannot be tempted with evil,
> neither tempteth he any man: But every man is
> tempted. (James 1:13–14a)

It is the imaginations of man that plague the mind so wickedly and cripple the believer's thoughts. It is here that the battle must be fought. And it must be fought with Scripture. As Scripture is learned, studied, and contemplated, the Holy Spirit will bring it to mind in order for the mind to submit itself to the Word and overcome the evil imaginations.

Self-condemnations, rejections, self-pity, thoughts of being unloved, unwanted, or unneeded, and feelings of failure always come from thought patterns in the mind more than from the realities of life. Our thought patterns, and our feelings stem from reactions, situations, or circumstances dealing with other people. They are vain imaginations. All people are consumed with themselves, for it is the disease of mankind. Other people are not concerned with us except in how it affects them. Outside of Jesus Christ, there is no caring for others. All caring outside of Jesus is totally self-oriented. This does not mean we should judge people harshly; we are people ourselves, but rather realizing this truth gives us a freedom from the bondage of man and man's approval for our life. Our personalities have been bruised but, by the precious blood of the Lamb, are made whole and healed. To grieve the Holy Spirit and lose His direction and edification leaves us vulnerable to mental anguish and pain. Consequently, as overcomers, we wish to learn not to grieve the Holy spirit in order that we are not left to be preyed upon by vain imaginations.

> Being filled with all unrighteousness, fornication,
> wickedness, covetousness, maliciousness; full of
> envy, murder, debate, deceit, malignity; whisper-
> ers, backbiters, haters of God, despiteful, proud,
> boasters, inventors of evil things, disobedient
> to parents, without understanding, covenant

breakers, without natural affection, implacable, unmerciful. (Romans 1:29–31)

This list of twenty-three human qualities describes how the believer grieves the Holy Spirit and brings about death in his own life, barring him from inheriting the kingdom of God. How quickly we love God and turn our entire being to Him when He reveals Himself to us and breathes the breath of life upon our being. With the baptism of the Holy Spirit, our love soars for the Father, and we are determined to give up all and follow Him with all of our heart. But then, how quickly we get confused and come to believe that our relationship with God is but a vertical one. While it is absolutely true that we must secure and possess a vertical relationship, without a horizontal relationship with our fellowman, the vertical relationship does not bear fruit. And we know that though eternal life is the gift of God, this is not His purpose for allowing us to live out our lives here. His purpose for our lives on earth is to magnify His name by living out our lives in His abiding presence. This is made possible by the Holy Spirit within us, His vessels. How much of God the world sees in us is dependent upon our willingness to allow Him to have His way through us. He is perfect and loves us. His way is always right and best. As believers, our actions, thoughts, words, motives, and in fact every aspect of our lives depict to this world of darkness that He truly lives and that God is God. We are His expression on earth!

We are God's ambassadors. The more we relinquish ourselves, the more He is able to abide and work through us. We have more power, His power. In rereading Romans 1:29–31, we see that every one of the traits listed deals with relationships regarding our fellowman. It is evident that we do not have a satisfactory vertical relationship unless our horizontal relationships with our fellowman show forth the love that God requires of us.

We love Him, because he first loved us. (1 John 4:19)

This is our vertical relationship.

> If a man say, I love God, and hateth his brother,
> he is a liar: for he that loveth not his brother
> whom he hath seen, how can he love God whom
> he hath not seen? (1 John 4:20)

This is our horizontal relationship. We must have the first in order to have the second. But if we do not live the second, we can question our relationship in the first. Our fruit is the outcome.

Now as followers and believers of Jesus Christ, we will not experience the approval of the world. And persecution shall be our companion, because the trust is an affront to mankind which he prefers to hide in the darkness.

> Blessed are ye, when men shall revile you, and
> persecute you, and shall say all manner of evil
> against you falsely, for my sake. (Matthew 5:11)

> And this is the condemnation, that light is come
> into the world, and men loved darkness rather
> than light, because their deeds were evil. (John
> 3:19)

So the love of God and the love of man through God is the truth of the Gospel. Consequently, we are not to judge ourselves with ourselves or to compare one to another but with the Word of God.

> For we dare not make ourselves of the number,
> or compare ourselves with some that commend
> themselves: but they measuring themselves by
> themselves, and comparing themselves among
> themselves, are not wise. (2 Corinthians 10:12)

All of us operate in the flesh from time to time. Relationships are difficult to work out. Even the flesh of our brothers and sisters in

Christ can be offended. People are ego against ego, will against will, pride against pride. We can, however, parallel our fullness of the presence of the Holy Spirit within us in accordance with the relationship and fellowship we have with our fellowman.

> When a man's ways please the Lord, he maketh
> even his enemies to be at peace with him.
> (Proverbs 16:7)

This does not mean we have no problems in relationships. Proverbs states that our enemies will be brought to peace, but enemies do exist. If we are pleasing to the world or to flesh, we are displeasing to God.

> Because the carnal mind is enmity against God:
> for it is not subject to the law of God, neither
> indeed can be. So then they that are in the flesh
> cannot please God. (Romans 8:7–8)

We Christians confront the world and flesh daily, especially our own!

Looking at Romans 1:29–31, we can see how our actions grieve the Holy Spirit. Remembered that as we move closer into the presence and heartbeat of our heavenly Father that the Holy Spirit speaks to us of those things that are offensive to God. Our motives must be pure. Each of the twenty-three human sins listed in Romans 1:29–31 deals with motives in regard to our relationship with other people. Man is seen as the sinful creature that he is, full of unrighteousness, doing anything and everything that will exalt himself even at the expense of others. Being consistently concerned with only himself and how he looks to everybody else is man's constant snare.

Our cruelty to others stems from attempting to protect ourselves. Or we are cruel as a means of expressing self-indulgence. We just don't "feel" like putting ourselves out for anyone else at that particular time and furthermore feel justified in being self-indulgent. Our Perizzites are death to us. Our thoughts need to be reined in so that we are thinking about what God has to say about any given situation. We need not let our thoughts just wander off in any direction. Remember, the Perizzites wandered and had no walls. We can choose to control our thoughts. It is difficult but can be accomplished by the power of Holy Spirit within us.

If we were able to obey God's commandments, we would not have to contend with our Perizzites, for each trait listed in Romans is against God's laws. The Perizzites are listed in Scripture in groups of tens and fives. God well knew that it would be impossible for man to obey His laws (ten is the biblical number for law), therefore we are covered by the grace of God (five is the biblical number for grace). As we break God's laws, allowing our minds to wander aimlessly, we fall into sin. We are always forgiven by the grace of God. But if we practice over and over to give our thoughts unto the Holy Spirit, we will find life more enjoyable and powerful. This is a daily walk, a taking up of our cross every day.

We find a remnant of the Perizzites in the court of Solomon, paying tribute to the king of Israel. Spiritually speaking, Solomon had control over the Perizzites, as the grace of God has the power over those flesh things we do and say to other people. Just as the Perizzites lived in unwalled cities and wandered, we let our thoughts wander and live in vain imaginations. So the Perizzites existed in Solomon's court; they had not been totally destroyed. We cannot control all of thoughts either, and they reign from time to time away from God. Unrighteousness, fornication, wickedness, covetousness, maliciousness, envy, murder, debate, deceit, malignity, whispering, backbiting, hatred of God, despitefulness, pride, boasting, invention of evil things, disobedience to parents, void of understanding, covenant breaking, heartlessness, being implacable, and unmerciful still exists. Given any flesh opportunity, they will rear their nasty head. Only in constant prayer, constant seeking, consistent repentance, and consistent relinquishment of our will to God's will can the Perizzites be kept under the blood of Jesus. Never is any saint so far along with God that they are not capable of earthly thoughts going wild. If this were not true, there would be no need for continued grace in mature Christians. Such Christians would be fulfilling the law. This is impossible; only Jesus fulfilled the law and the requirements thereof. He is grace.

> Think not that I am come to destroy the law, or
> the prophets: I am not come to destroy, but to
> fulfill. (Matthew 5:17)

Our mind is of this world and must be trained and renewed constantly. Our soul, though it will live eternally, is tarnished by the world. Our Perizzites dwell within us, feeling totally justified in their actions. We strike out to hurt from our own hurts and feelings by allowing our souls to be "open dwellers" or possessed by the Perizzites and not curtailing our thoughts we suffer.

Our Jesus-filled spirits are given the task of urging our souls into the obedience of the cross in order that the abundant life can be secured. God has placed us in a giant school—life. How quickly we progress is dependent on how quickly we die to ourselves and obey the Holy Spirit's urgings and direction. We must have God's Word within us in order for the Holy Spirit to bring it up to us.

> But the Comforter, which is the Holy Ghost,
> whom the Father will send in my name, he shall
> teach you all things, and bring all things to your
> remembrance, whatsoever I have said unto you.
> (John 14:26)

In order to be obedient to the voice of God, we must know it is the voice of God. The more of God's Word that dwells within us, the more easily we can decipher His voice over the voice of Satan or our own voice. As we sin, the verse against that sin will immediately be brought to our minds, and we can then repent and learn. If we think upon sin, the Holy Spirit will also bring to mind Scripture against that thought, and we can avoid sin by being obedient. To know His Word then is to know life. There is so much we do not know, and God reveals His desire to us daily as we follow and worship Him. It is a daily walk, a daily enlightenment. There is that time for learning then the testing of our newly acquired knowledge, that gaining of experience and then the moving into a rest. Each step is God-ordered. Our part, is willingness. He does it all.

In summary, we choose on what we will think about. Perizzites unwalled lives are open for all kinds of evil thoughts and vain imaginations. Our souls are Perizzites, letting any and all kinds of thoughts to enter in. We protect our souls with the Word of God. Thinking about God and His Word prevents us from vain imaginations, protects our minds from wandering to thoughts of sin and then committing sin.

Chapter 10

The Girgashites

And Joshua said, Hereby ye shall know that
the living God is among you, and that he
will without fail drive out from before you
the Canaanites, and the Hittites, and the
Hivites, and the Perizzites, and the Girgashites,
and the Amorites, and the Jebusites.

—Joshua 3:10

The next tribe to be discussed is the Girgashites. They are listed only seven times in Scripture. There is no indication of their definite locality; however, it is believed that they were dwellers on clayey soil. The most interesting historical fact about the Girgashites is that they were totally destroyed by the Israelites. No remnant of them is mentioned in Scripture.

Being mentioned only seven times in Scripture and the fact that these people were destroyed gives the Girgashites a unique soulish parallel for us in our spiritual walk. Biblically, the number seven means completeness, and perfection. The fact that these people were totally destroyed is also indicative that this work accomplished by the Holy Spirit in us is complete and conclusive.

As the believer matures in Christ Jesus, a deepening revelation of who and what Jesus did for mankind comes into focus. As babes, baptized in the Holy Spirit, our entire life is centered on Jesus Christ and what He has done for us. As the maturing process begins and the Holy Spirit begins to unveil us to ourselves, that initial giddiness subsides. The dying of self has begun, and pain to the believer comes in, as it is painful to the flesh to die. Again, the soul must subject itself to the guidance of the Spirit and transform the mind to the thoughts of Christ.

Maturation brings about many changes for the believer. If the Holy Spirit is given free rein, the changes are all for good. Yet even as the vessel is changing and becoming more like the image of Jesus, too many successes cause the flesh to feel it has improved. Pride comes about, and the vessel is again in sin. God allows trials, tribulations, and sufferings to come about to actually protect the believer from his worst enemy—himself. For our own pride is destructive and will ultimately separate us from our Beloved, as He, and He only, is worthy of praise and honor. We are merely vessels of clay, but how quickly we forget. It is God's love for us that He teaches us obedience through our sufferings.

> Though he were a Son, yet learned he obedience
> by the things which he suffered. (Hebrews 5:8)

So we grow through our trials; always there is a balance; for we also experience tremendous blessings and spiritual triumphs. But if these become the norm for us, we can forget who does it all and fall into the sin trap of thinking we somehow have accomplished something. Even the more mature Christian will sometimes carry his "accomplishments" to the altar and offer them to God, thinking this, in some way, pleases the Father. Our blessings and triumphs become a snare. There is no work we can do. It is always the grace of God, His work, His accomplishment, His will through us, the vessel He Himself has chosen and is making into His image. Whether we eventually take credit for what we have done or whether we attempt to pass on our victories to the Father, both concepts and behavior are wrong, for He does it all.

This is our Girgashite, thinking we can do anything for God. There must be a total realization that God does all in all. He is complete. He is perfect. As His creation, we must allow total death to self's accomplishments and victories and understand that Jesus has finished it all.

> As Jesus said in his last breathe:
> It is finished. (John 19:30)

This is God's way. And our part is as it has always been, relinquishing our wills to His.

> But now, O Lord, thou art our father; we are the
> clay, and thou our potter; and we all are the work
> of thy hand. (Isaiah 64:8)

The Girgashites were people who made their home on clayey soil. As Christians, we abide with the Potter only because we were clay, chosen to do so. How can there be pride when the Potter chooses and the clay becomes what the Potter has preordained for the clay to be. Nonetheless, our pride rises; and inevitably, we forget that we are but clay. After accepting that we are clay, our pride is such that we even exalt ourselves for being the clay the Potter chose. Our feeling should be one of humility and a fear of the Lord. We ought to be eternally grateful and thankful for God, choosing such a vessel as ourselves for His everlasting abiding.

It is evident from Scripture that God is no respecter of persons and that He loves all the same. While this is eternally true, it is equally true that He chooses us and that we do not choose Him.

> Ye have not chosen me, but I have chosen you,
> and ordained you, that ye should go and bring
> forth fruit, and that your fruit should remain:
> that whatsoever ye shall ask of the Father in my
> name, he may give it you. (John 15:16)

He alone knows the heart that He has prepared to abide with Him and in Him. As we follow Jesus Christ and come to this understanding, a humility will begin to grow in our inner man. Remembering that the Girgashites are overcome and totally destroyed, we can, as created beings, know that He has overcome all for us, and everything is in Him. We begin to see His sovereignty and find we can accept life in a different way than before. The yoke, though present, is easy. And the burden, though real, is light; and we pass our cares onto Him who is able to carry them.

> Casting all your care upon him; for he careth for
> you. (1 Peter 5:7)

And just as we give Him our cares, so also are we able to give Him the glory that is His. By His grace, and His grace alone, we are able to live for Him. He lives in us, enabling us to do that which we are unable to do without Him.

God gave mankind the law. It was because of the law that man then recognized sin. Had man been able to obey the law, the law itself would have been sufficient to ensure mankind eternal life. The law of God, which was given for life to man, was in reality death for man. The law showed man his sin, and the wages of sin are death, and sin separates man from God. So instead of the law giving life to man, it pronounced death upon him. The law itself however is just, holy, and good. It is man that is evil. It is not that the law is unjust. It is just that man is unable to obey the law. Even those few who desire to obey the law also find it impossible to do so. The nature of man is at enmity with the law, and man does what is against the law of God even as he wishes to obey the law.

> Because the carnal mind is enmity against God:
> for it is not subject to the law of God, neither
> indeed can be. (Romans 8:7)

So man discovers that it is impossible for him to please his Creator, for he is unable to be obedient to the law. Whether man finds the law good or fair is unimportant, for God presented the law to man to be obeyed. There is nothing man can do in works, in attitude, in accomplishments, in any "doings" whatsoever that fulfill perfect obedience to the law. Therefore, at this point, man is separated from His Creator.

> But your inquities have separated between you
> and your God, and your sins have hid his face
> from you, that he will not hear. (Isaiah 59:2)

One of the most difficult concepts of truth for man to understand is that God is truly God and that He did truly create all things.

> Through faith we understand that the worlds
> were framed by the word of God, so that things
> which are seen were not made of things which do
> appear. (Hebrews 11:3)

Therefore, as being formed out of things that had not yet appeared until our Creator spoke them into existence, it must be understood that the Creator holds final authority on everything that exists because He spoke it into being in the first place. When God states what is good, that is what is good, not what we may think is good. When God states what love is, that is love, not what we think love is. When God states what is sin, that is sin, not what we call sin. To be given the gift of eternal life is how God planned it to be given, not how we think it should be. It is truly ludicrous to think of the thing created, arguing with the Creator, and yet that is exactly what we human beings do.

Since God created all, what God says, is. Good is good only because God ordains it as good. All God does is good, holy, and perfect, for He is good, holy, and perfect. He chooses His vessels because it pleases Him, not because obedience to the law has been fulfilled. Without His indwelling power, the vessel cannot be obedient to the law.

> Therefore hath he mercy on whom he will have mercy, and whom he will he hardeneth. Thou wilt say then unto me, Why doth he yet find fault? For who hath resisted his will? Nay but, O man, who are thou that repliest against God? Shall the thing formed say to him that formed it, Why hast thou made me thus? (Romans 9:18–20)

There is nothing we have done or could do. God does it all.

> For whom he did foreknow, he also did predestinate to be conformed to the image of his Son, that he might be the first-born among many brethren. Moreover whom he did predestinate, them he also called: and whom he called, them he also justified: and whom he justified, them he also glorified. (Romans 8:29–30)

Such a spiritual truth, permeating into our inner being, brings continual praise to our Father and continual thanksgiving. Remember, He is the Creator. He is good, perfect, holy, and true God. He chose the perfect way for us to attain what He has for us without our doing anything. He breathes His breath of life upon us, and then He chooses to indwell us with His Spirit. His Spirit then leads us into those things that are best for us. We become more and more pliable vessels, worshipping the perfect and righteous God. Giving us Himself is life itself! He is perfect. Thereby, His plan is perfect.

Like the people who chose to live on clay, the Girgashities, we relinquish our wills to the Potter and become like clay. We are then fashioned into that wonderful vessel that the Potter has ordained for us from the beginning of time.

Chapter 11

The Amorites

The Amorite tribes were never totally destroyed by the Israelites. The Amorite people were giantlike in size and were referred to as the mountain people. As mountain people, these tribes controlled formidable land areas next to Jerusalem itself that prevented the Hebrews from any total victory. They are mentioned over seventy-five times in the Bible, indicating their continual presence throughout the years of Israel's ancient history.

> But the Amorites would dwell in Mount Heres in Aijalon, and in Shaalbim: yet the hand of the house of Joseph prevailed, so that they became tributaries. (Judges 1:35)

As tributaries, these people were like winding threads that appeared over and again throughout Israel's history of conquest as an ancient nation. And though never completely destroyed, they were kept under control by the Jews. Thus, the story from without is that the Amorites were continuously a literal thorn in the flesh to the Jews who were attempting to reenter and conquer all of Palestine.

In the Spirit, Amorites represent our old nature. They are the old man. He must be placed on the cross with day-to-day relinquishment. And like the tribe itself, the old man reoccurs throughout our lifetime. With each outburst of our old nature, it is like a mountain that is not easily overcome. In fact, there is no indication in Scripture that our old nature or our Amorite is destroyed. He is a stronghold within us, like mountains, not pliable at all. But praise God, our Amorite is placed under the blood of Jesus Christ. Our sins are forgiven by Jesus upon repentance. As we contend with our old man, we must continue over and over to regenerate our minds with the Word of God and work out those constant snares within our being. We are forced to recognize our old man from time to time as he makes himself known in unwanted outbursts. But seeing ourselves in this light gives us compassion for our fellowman and reminds us that we too are human.

Our old nature is made up of a multitude of personality traits that continue to plague the Christian throughout our lifetime as we continually repent and renew our strength at the cross. The Amorites within our own personalities are as numerous as the Amorites who continually rose up against the Hebrews. Giants are so large; we cannot see them ourselves. Just as a forest cannot be seen for the trees, we cannot see all those things that make up our own old nature. They loom inside of us, and only when defined by the Holy Spirit can we see them.

Amorites, as our old nature, when correctly agitated, irritated, or frustrated, explode into total flesh behavior, our flesh surfaces, and we react as we have always reacted. Though we feel justified at the time in our actions, we are later dismayed that we are so capable of behaving like we did before we decided to earnestly follow Jesus. To an onlooker, it appears that our so-called 'Christianity' is truly just full of holes. Our new life in Jesus appears to have no validity at all, and we are criticized as one of those who can talk the talk but not walk the walk. But many times, this Christian is most assuredly changed and is walking the walk. It is just, at this particular time, the sin nature comes forth. Flesh will resurrect itself periodically, depending on the amount of pressure applied to it. It does not make such behavior right, but it is a very real occurrence in the Christian's life.

Christians are not perfect. They are being conformed. This process takes a lifetime. Some areas are more easily relinquished than others. Outwardly, easily detected sins may be given up immediately.

Hidden jealousy, on the other hand, takes a lifetime. Outbursts of temper, judgmental statements, ego justifications, manipulations, desire for power, prestige, money, and recognition of self are not traits that die easily. Consequently, when enough pressure is exerted upon the believer, self surfaces. Those around the believer suffer, but most of all, for the one who has purposed to give his life to Jesus Christ, the Amorites represent a great thorn in the flesh. It is one thing to admit to self and selfish desires. It is quite another thing to see them in operation when one wants to do the right thing.

> For the good that I would I do not: but the evil
> which I would not, that I do. Now if I do that
> I would not, it is no more I that do it, but sin
> that dwelleth in me. I find then a law, that when
> I would do good, evil is present with me. For I
> delight in the law of God after the inward man.
> (Romans 7:19–22)

The constant quip, "I thought he was supposed to be a Christian," is usually heard when an Amorite has raised his head. A Christian to the non-Christian world is a person who claims to be perfect and has no faults. Furthermore, he is always to be agreeable and do what the other person wants, or he is not behaving like a Christian. The less mature Christian feels exactly the same way. What he expects from others, he does not feel he must do himself. In fact, this Christian cannot see the giants in his life. They loom so large; they blind his eyes, and his growth in this area will be stagnant. He denies any possibility that past flesh behavior can still react.

To the immature Christian, or the believer who is satisfied where he is, Amorites are things that hurt other Christians' witness but not his. If this believer fails, he quickly justifies himself in such a way that his failing is not failure at all. If he has behaved in a wrathful way, his feeling is that anyone would have gotten mad in such a situation, and furthermore, he had not been so mad in a long time anyway. He too may justify his flesh anger by defining it as "righteousness indignation." This person can also convince himself that he did not behave poorly at all but was very much in control, merely seething within. And hadn't he come a long way for he was no longer screaming without? But Christians bottling up these tendencies have not grasped the meaning of the Gospel at all. God is always concerned with the heart and how it responds and feels. False behavior brings about a self-righteousness that is not of God at all. Self-righteousness brings about a feeling of false humility, and the Christian becomes very judgmental of others. He is also an authority on all things. This intolerance becomes quite unbearable for others around him.

The immature Christian honestly believes he has arrived within the ranks of perfection and can fairly judge all others around him in all circumstances. These types of people are overbearing with no humor in life about themselves, believing they are above it all. In groups, they cause tenseness as others around them, feel their judgments without them having said a word. Such persons honestly believe that whatever traits they once had, they are now walking in the divine light and are no longer like the rest of the human race. Such a poor, poor witness this individual really is. Yet he is blinded to himself, feeling the rest of the world is totally out of step, and he and he alone has conquered life with all its faults. His secret sins remain just that, and he continues his facade to the tiring of those around him and eventually to the tiring of himself. A leavening inevitably takes place, and some such souls go back to their lives before Christianity. This does not mean they lose their salvation, just the abundant life in the here and now. Others remain caught in their own web of misery and self-condemnation. Their judgment of others in accordance with God's law of reciprocity eventually falls upon themselves, and their life becomes void of joy.

> Therefore thou art inexcusable, O man, whosoever thou art that judgest: for wherein thou judgest another, thou condemnest thyself; for thou that judgest doest the same things. (Romans 2:1)

Practicing only a part of the Gospel robs these individuals. Our churches are full of such Christians. Our doctrines and theologies are full of don'ts and do nots! We become strangled by Christianity instead of freed.

Think not however that the more mature Christian is immune to his Amorites, For one thing it must remembered that Amorites are giants and not conquerable. They exist within us, just as they remained with the Israelites. In fact, one aspect of maturity is admitting to the truth that Amorites exist. For the Christian who has made Jesus Christ not only Savior but Lord of his life, Amorites may not resurrect as often, but completely dead, they are not. The mature believer abhors his Amorites but knows they are there. He knows that he himself has not improved, that flesh is flesh. He fully understands that minute-by-minute repentance is necessary. He is more aware of his pitfalls in the world and attempts to remove himself from such situations and circumstances. He is studying the Word, praising and worshipping the Father. This believer is more tolerant than any other Christian. He comprehends the Gospel and realizes that perfection is not for us in this life. He allows for the mistakes of others. He attempts to see things from their point of view, knowing that he too is as full of flesh as those he is judging. He understands that flesh is going to be flesh from time to time and that remaining in the spirit 100 percent of the time is not possible. He continuously rejoices in the forgiveness of sins and praises God for the atoning blood of Jesus Christ. This believer knows the blood accomplishes what he is unable to ever accomplish. He is by far society's greatest witness. For in his effort to please God, he is not attempting to be a witness for man's sake but rather attempting to live the Gospel because of his love for Jesus Christ. Because of his revelation of the Gospel, he realizes that Amorites are real and that, with the right amount of pressure, he will respond in the flesh as he always has, as if there were no Jesus.

Yet realizing this truth and experiencing it are poles apart. The grace of God we can accept in others, but we find it difficult to accept in ourselves. In maturing, we find we can forgive others for their Amorites. But sometimes, in our own failings, we want to believe we are conquered, and we are perfect. Such a rendezvous with self we lived in. Finally able to allow others to have failings, we want perfection of ourselves. Self desires to have no need of grace. With the need of grace, there is no self-exaltation. Thus, to fall to our own Amorite generally causes great self-condemnation. We always feel within ourselves, we can achieve alone while the Bible says we must have grace in order to follow Jesus Christ.

Amorites therefore are blessings in our lives. They come as curses. They appear to absolutely devastate us. We find ourselves feeling and behaving as we did before we had ever given our lives to Jesus Christ. When such old familiar traits arise in our personalities, we, above all, are shocked at our own behavior. In theory, we can discuss Amorites and realize that every person has many giants in their lives. Our own Amorites however can be invisible to us. We are blinded by the enormity of the giant, until the Holy Spirit reveals it to us.

But our Amorites are a blessing to us. No matter how far we grow in Jesus, no matter how much we study His Word and do all the things we may believe matter, the outburst of an Amorite reminds us that we are just human. We are not above the remaining human race or special in any way. We are born-again creations, vessels of clay being fashioned into the likeness of our brother, Jesus. It is good to see ourselves as we are in the flesh. How blessed we are to be born again and to know the Lord Jesus Christ and to be walking in the Spirit. How blessed we are too to fall periodically so as to be reminded of who we are and who He is. Ah, we need the grace of God so, and if not reminded of it from time to time, we do forget. Our Amorites help to keep us humble. They chip away tremendously at our pride. For this reason, they are indeed a blessing. Our pride is our greatest enemy against God, so failure is a great tool that comes to us with love from the Father. In failure, we realize who we still are. Without grace, there would be no life of peace, no life of joy, no life.

Failure brings about pain and causes us to reevaluate our situation and our reaction. Justification is of no avail. Repentance is our only recourse. The spiritual man who has behaved carnally and allowed the Amorite to surface now must repent for his error. How humbling repentance is. Repentance in itself is repugnant to the carnal man for he wishes to believe that he is perfect and finds no reason for repenting. And yet, as it is with all things of the Spirit, this capitulation to the realization of the Amorite and the need for repentance brings about spiritual growth. True humility is practiced, and this act in itself brings more light into the individual's character. The light brings about more peace, joy, and love. How perfect our Father's plan consistently remains to be?—failures, yes, but made into victories by God. To the world, such victory is not visible. Only the outburst of the Amorite is remembered. But again, this fact too is humbling to the believer as he so wanted to look good to the world. But God has never been concerned with our image to the world. His only concern is our inner man being made into His likeness. As the inner man grows in Jesus Christ, the outer man responds. So what looks like defeat to the world is actually victory for the Christian. Humility replaces haughtiness. Meekness overcomes self-assertion. And godliness overpowers wickedness. None such virtues are appealing to the flesh or to the world. The world says sacrifice all else if necessary but never self. But for the chosen Christian, self has to be the sacrifice.

Amorites are different things to different people. What would be an Achilles' heel to one would matter not to another. This is the reason we judge so profusely. Why? We would never behave in such a manner as we see a brother doing. Christians are very hard on one another, demanding a standard they never impose upon themselves, for generally, they believe they have overcome in that area. We must be ever mindful however that any variance from the law is as if we broke the whole law. There are no degrees of sin.

> For whosoever shall keep the whole law, and yet offend in one point, he is guilty of all. (James 2:10)

There are some Amorites or giants in life that are common to all man, though all man may not recognize them. Our culture is an Amorite. There are many things we believe and have absorbed into our thought patterns by just being alive and living in and around things about us. We assume such mores, folkways, habits, and customs to be right when in fact they may not be right at all. As people raised in a particular culture and literally trained by osmosis to believe and feel and respond in certain modes of behavior, the idea of right or wrong is not even the question. One merely tries to fit into his environment, find recognition and acceptance by playing the rules of the game. Jesus Christ fits no mold of behavior acceptable to the world and its rules. He has overcome the world, much to its dismay. We are called to do the same. Thus, to discover what we have always been taught to be right is now wrong is quite a shock. With Jesus, we learn a new and better way to respond or react to a particular situation. We must relinquish our absolutes. Our finality on a subject may be entirely wrong and a whole new learning process may be required before we can see the truth that Jesus has for us for any given situation at any given time.

However even as we practice such, we find that our past heritage will arise periodically in our thought patterns and overtake us. We find ourselves believing and saying the same things we always believed and said before we learned differently in Jesus. Such behavior is the occurrence of an Amorite. Amorites are as old as we are, causing us to drag our culture with us, whether we want it or not. To completely free ourselves of our culture is impossible. We must place Amorites under the blood of Jesus. But as we, as believers, fall in the flesh, an Amorite will raise his head, standing on the ground of traditions. The traditions of man are strong ties, not easily broken. Our traditions are such a part of us that it is as if something sacred has been attacked when they are even challenged.

Another Amorite in the life of a believer deals with his family. We are taught so much from our family. We derive our self-worth from our upbringing. Everything we are and have become from our own family, we then take into our marriage. We have an immense number of problems that have been with us since childhood. Yet we are fiercely loyal to our own particular family background. Good or bad, we relive our past in our marriages. We fight to prove our family's ways and attitudes were the best. What we were taught as children is ingrained in us. We act out our behavior learned from childhood, not even aware of the snare we live in. Much of the way we feel and say are Hivites, those sins we are not even aware of. In fact, those things we abhor the most and determine never to do or be seem to have an invisible hold upon us. Most of the time, we are not even aware of our family Amorites. We cannot express our hurts or frustrations, for they are deeply embedded within our makeup, needing the healing power of the blood of Jesus.

Within families certain behavior is expected, a mode of behavior has been established for each family member, and any change is greeted with skepticism. A born-again creature is a new creature. The Christian who wants a deeper walk with the Lord is changing, but families expect certain modes of behavior, and it is actually an invisible umbilical cord that links us to old patterns, in spite of our new nature. We feel pulled in a direction that we no longer wish to go. We thought we would no longer feel that particular way. When this happens, we should recognize these as Amorites, familiar patterns, like old shoes luring us into habits we had hoped were long since passed. This causes problems for children with parents. The child, regardless of the age, seems to revert back in many ways in the presence of the parent. All the years and patterns are in conflict with any new behavior or response.

When an Amorite arises in this Christian, he is immediately judged and told that he has not changed at all. The outburst of the old man is devastating to the believer. This is why it is difficult for one family member to walk on a new plane with the Lord while other family members are blinded to His truths. However, we know that Jesus is aware of this.

As Christians, we must confront our selfishness, see and confess our utter dependence on Jesus Christ. For without Him, we are lost, not only eternally but here in this world. Even an unbeliever is disgusted with total flesh outbursts that reveal man's base nature, for the entire world system is made up of ways to hide and then justify selfish desires and motives. Many Christians remain in the world system, deceiving themselves as to their true nature. Forgiveness and repentance are the key: "more of Jesus, less of me."

Chapter 12

The Jebusites

As for the Jebusites the inhabitants of Jerusalem,
the children of Judah could not drive them
out: but the Jebusites dwell with the children
of Judah at Jerusalem unto this day.
—Joshua 15:63

The name of Jerusalem under the control of the Jebusites was called Jebus or "trodden under foot." Of all the tribes that the Israelites had confronted, the Jebusites, though not the most vicious, were the vilest in moral character. They were widely known as the people whose moral fiber was degenerate and base. Their sexual behavior ranged from homosexuality to bestiality with no compunction whatsoever. It was as if God looked upon the earth for the place where there was no goodness at all and said that will be my chosen place above all the earth.

It is His perfection to take the worst, for with His light, it then is made into the best. At the time of the division of the land of Canaan, Jerusalem was given to the tribe of Benjamin.

And the children of Benjamin did not drive out
the Jebusites that inhabited Jerusalem; but the
Jebusites dwell with the children of Benjamin in
Jerusalem unto this day. (Judges 1:21)

Jerusalem means foundation of shalom or peace. Jehovah-Jireh means "Lord will provide," and the Lord provided in Scripture for Jerusalem to be the city of peace as He Himself will abide there. It was David who defeated the Jebusites and took the city. David defeated them by cutting off their water supply.

> Nevertheless David took the stronghold of Zion:
> the same is the city of David. (2 Samuel 5:7)

If the water supply is cut out of our life, we die. God's Word is our water supply. If we choose to ignore it and not believe it, we live dead and die separated from God for all eternity. The Jebusites were not totally annihilated because the children of Israel were not able to do so.

The Jebusites represent the very core of our being. All seven tribes discussed are types of our soulish traits and behavior. But it is the Jebusites that inhabit the center of our being. All other tribes must be defeated or overcome before Jerusalem can be entered into. Jerusalem is symbolic of "self," and all self represents. For all our personality traits are there to protect self, the ego. The entire world system is based on the order of protecting self. Every worldly institution is built upon the premise of self and the protection thereof. Christianity is repugnant to self because Christ calls for its death.

> And he said to them all, if any man will come
> after me, let him deny himself, and take up his
> cross daily, and follow me. For whosoever will
> save his life shall lose it: but whosoever will lose
> his life for my sake, the same shall save it. For
> what is a man advantaged, if he gain the whole
> world, and lose himself, or be cast away? (Luke
> 9:23–25)

Self feels rejected. It is this fact that causes all people to do anything to give self the feeling that it has worth and importance. Rejection was conceived in the womb because of the original sin of

Adam. The only man ever born without the spirit of rejection was Jesus. And because all people feel rejected, it is inevitable that we reject one another as our own judgment falls upon ourselves, and we do to others what has been done unto us.

The entire world is set upon a course of destruction, causing pain and suffering to one another as self attempts to be protected, guarded, and nurtured. We are all aware of our insatiable hunger to edify ourselves or receive exaltation. In a group picture, the first person we seek out is ourselves. Our thoughts are always upon ourselves, and we feel that everything that happens involves us. Every action another person takes that is within our own realm, we believe, is directed toward us or against us. We profess brotherhood, but selfhood is our real interest.

For the Christian, this self must be dealt with and given a fatal blow, or the deeper Christian walk is impossible. As self decreases, the presence of Jesus increases in our lives. As John the Baptist said, "He must increase, but I must decrease" (John 3:30). The spirit that surrounds self in order to justify all its actions is jealousy. Jealousy permeates the body of Christ today worse than any other malady. Jealousy coats self as with an outer covering. It is out of jealousy that we judge our fellow brothers and sisters in the Lord. It is out of jealousy that we can put ourselves above others, claiming we have certain knowledge or wisdom that is yet hidden to their eyes. And essentially, it is this feeling of jealousy that is at the core of our being. We feel offended if we do not get whatever it is that we want or feel we have a right to have. We expect other people to pour their lives into our lives, while at the same time, they expect the same thing from us.

So man has invented all types of games that all know how to play in order to hide the vulnerability of self. We say and do things in order to hide our real feelings, for if such feelings were shared, then self would be injured. Our thought patterns move into imaginations totally consumed in thought of self. Self is that center of all that is evil, for it is only interested in self. Everything else is of no interest if self cannot be satisfied. Just as the Jebusites located in the center of the promised land are the most wicked of all the tribes, so is self, our inner core, the center of all our wickedness.

There are no bounds that an ego will not go to in order to satisfy itself. If the ego is bruised badly enough, there are no rules that will not be broken nor commitments too sacred to be sacrificed in order to justify self. Self knows no reason or truth; only the satisfying of itself is its concern. The Bible teaches us that man is not even aware of his evilness and protection of himself. In fact, many people are duped into believing that they are good and are motivated to do for others. The Bible teaches us just the opposite, that without the infilling and indwelling of the Spirit of God, we are not capable of doing any good or of bettering self.

The closer we move into the throne room and into an intimate relationship with Jesus Christ, the more aware of our sins we become. Our sin of self over God, and love of self over anyone and anything else is laid naked before us. We continually fall upon the cross, the more we love our Savior for what He has done.

Another aspect of self is that it is totally destructive. We are doomed to destroy ourselves, for regardless of how we may feel about things, God is in control. God's laws are absolute. There is no altering them or changing them. He establishes the way man must live, and any variance from God's eternal plan brings about consequences. These consequences are destructive to self. We can either relinquish self and receive God's blessings or ignore God's call for the death of self and suffer loss. God is totally sovereign, and being outside of obedience to His Word brings about repercussions that result with each disobedience. There is a sowing and reaping principle in the world that is irreversible and absolute.

> Be not deceived: God is not mocked: for whatsoever a man soweth, that shall he also reap. For he that soweth to his flesh shall of the flesh reap corruption; but he that soweth to the Spirit shall of the Spirit reap life everlasting. And let us not be weary in well doing: for in due season we shall reap, if we faint not. (Galatians 6:7–9)

In Deuteronomy chapter 29, the curses are listed that befall man as he turns from God and follows his own selfish desires.

Because flesh is flesh and man is man, it is impossible to change our nature even if man desired to do so. We find ourselves in a plight. Even born again and desiring God, we find that to deny ourselves is not something that operates automatically within us. With the baptism of the Holy Spirit, we become acutely aware of the spiritual world and our relationship to it. Yet even with the baptism of the Holy Spirit, the conquering of self looms upon us.

It must be understood here that we do not speak of salvation. What is spoken of here is that deeper walk, that minute-by-minute communion with the Lord Jesus Christ. The utter commitment and desire is to be like Jesus, to taste what He tasted in order that our image be conformed into His. Oh, how many different types of children our Father has? And how He loves them all for He Himself came up with the varieties. It is our sovereign God who allows different growths for His many varied children. All are loved equally by the Father. But there is that group of believers who are never satisfied, who constantly hunger, who desire incessantly to look inward and take more and more to the cross. To die to self is ultimate life to this believer. He desires to pay the price as he knows that new Jerusalem, the center core, is indeed the resting place of Jesus Christ Himself.

May it be said here that since our God is sovereign, He alone chooses which saints will take this deeper walk. It is not our intent to prove or disprove that truth here. It is however to be remembered that if such a saint is chosen, he is not special and more loved. He is however chosen because it pleased our Father to do so. This fact alone brings such a believer to his knees, often in utter praise and thanksgiving. This believer will taste a higher freedom only known to those who relinquish self. And such a relinquishment of self involves a dying that is impossible outside of an intimate relationship with the Holy Spirit. It is the Spirit's purpose to bring us into the full realization of who Jesus Christ is. The Spirit of God teaches us that we may receive what God has for us. It must be remembered that our flesh is at enmity with the things of God, and to deny self, even for glory to God, is a very difficult thing to do.

And when he (the Spirit) is come, he will reprove
the world of sin, and of righteousness, and of
judgement: Of sin, because they believe not on
me; Of righteousness, because I go to my Father,
and ye see me no more; Of judgement, because
the prince of this world is judged. I have yet many
things to say unto you, but ye cannot bear them
now. Howbeit when he, the Spirit of truth, is
come, he will guide you into all truth: for he shall
not speak of himself; but whatsoever he shall hear
that shall he speak: and he will show you things
to come. He shall glorify me: for he shall receive
of mine, and shall show it unto you. All things
that the Father hath are mine: therefore said I,
that he shall take of mine, and shall show it unto
you. (John 16:8–15)

Being confident of this very thing, that he which
hath begun a good work in you will perform it
until the day of Jesus Christ. (Philippians 1:6)

To wish to die to self is a thought of the heart placed there by
the power of the Holy Spirit. It certainly is not the desire of our flesh
nor is it the desire of an unregenerated mind.

Because the carnal mind is enmity against God:
for it is not subject to the law of God, neither
indeed can be. So then they that are in the flesh
cannot please God. (Romans 8:7–8)

We are not good and do not desire to be good in the godly
sense, so the presence of the Holy Spirit within us must continuously
carry us to death of self. Dying to self means relinquishing all of our
"rights" or those things we feel we deserve because we are alive. We
must forfeit all recognition, admiration, power, prestige, and social
position. Flesh must be willing not to exalt itself. This is an impossi-

ble task without the constant renewing of the mind and an attitude of repentance wrapped about in humility. The flesh rises up, and the mind justifies our actions so quickly that we find we truly are in a twenty-four-hour battle. And only to the believer who has determined to live such a crucified life can the joy be expressed because it is this plan that the Father intended for the church. It is when such a mode of living is walked out daily that life—and life abundant—is experienced. There is no other life. Trials, tribulations, suffering, and adverse circumstances become challenges, fully realizing that the victory on the other side is more than worth the price that self is asked to pay.

> For I know that in me (that is, in my flesh,) dwelleth no good thing: for to will is present with me; but how to perform that which is good I find not. For the good that I would I do not: but the evil which I would not, that I do. Now if I do that I would not, it is no more I that do it, but sin that dwelleth in me. I find then a law, that, when I would do good, evil is present with me. For I delight in the law of God after the inward man: But I see another law in my members, warring against the law of my mind, and bringing me into captivity to the law of sin which is in my members. O wretched man that I am! who shall deliver me from the body of this death? I thank God through Jesus Christ our Lord. So then with the mind I myself serve the law of God; but with the flesh the law of sin. (Romans 7:18–25)

We find then that our flesh is totally consumed in self, and our mind and our spirit need to be brought into the obedience of Jesus Christ.

> And be not conformed to this world: but be ye transformed by the renewing of your mind, that

ye may prove what is that good, and acceptable,
and perfect, will of God. (Romans 12:2)

In order then to die to self, we must be obedient to God's Word. We cannot, but we can saturate our minds with God's Word, then the Word itself crucifies self.

For the word of God is quick, and powerful, and
sharper than any two-edged sword, piercing even
to the dividing asunder of soul and spirit, and
of the joints and marrow, and is a discerner of
the thoughts and intents of the heart. (Hebrews
4:12)

As we are seeking God's Word, reading it, meditating upon it, memorizing it, it miraculously becomes a part of us.

This book of the law shall not depart out of thy
mouth; but thou shalt meditate therein day and
night, that thou mayest observe to do according
to all that is written therein: for then thou shalt
make thy way prosperous, and then thou shalt
have good success. (Joshua 1:8)

And it shall come to pass, if thou shalt hearken
diligently unto the voice of the Lord thy God, to
observe and to do all his commandments which
I command thee this day, that the Lord thy God
will set thee on high above all nations of the
earth. (Deuteronomy 28:1)

But his delight is in the law of the Lord; and in
his law doth he meditate day and night. (Psalm
1:2)

> My son, forget not my law; but let thine heart keep my commandments. (Proverbs 3:1)

God's commandment is quite simple.

> And Jesus said unto him, Thou shalt love the Lord thy God with all thy heart, and with all thy soul, and with all thy mind. This is the first and great commandment. And the second is like unto it, Thou shalt love thy neighbor as thyself. On these two commandments hang all the law and prophets. (Matthew 22:37–40)

First, we are to love God with all our heart, soul, and mind. Our spirit is already in love with God as He dwells within us. But the rest of our makeup must choose God over self. We can only die to self as we put His Word in our heart, meditate on it in our mind, and renew our souls with the truth. The healing and dying must come by the Spirit of God. We can do nothing to change except relinquish to the Master's hand.

The second step is the obvious outcome of the first, as we love God above all else, then loving our neighbor is the natural outcome. We no longer are seeking our own interest and desires at heart but are now concerned with others. For the heart of God is consumed with all of mankind. And as we relinquish ourselves to God and love Him best, we are then conforming to His nature. It is a process, a daily process, that begins with preference of others over ourselves. The dying to self is a lifetime step-by-step commitment into the likeness of our Father carried out by the power of the Holy Spirit through the grace of our Lord and Savior, Jesus Christ. Hallelujah!

Chapter 13

The Cost of Self

Jerusalem, at last! Canaan land was secured. The Israelites had returned home. It would appear the battle was won and a, carefree life was now awaiting the Jew. But of course, historically, this was not what happened at all. The land was secure only by continuous battling for it. Judges were raised up as both military leaders and rulers of the land. But rulership by judges was short-lived as the people cried out for a king. Israel's three kings, Saul, David, and Solomon, reigned, then Israel was divided into the northern and southern kingdoms. First and Second Kings and First and Second Chronicles portray Israel's life with her dual kingdoms and kings. The southern kingdom, Judah, and the northern kingdom, Israel, fought amongst themselves. Disobedience to God brought about foreign captivity of both kingdoms. Assyria defeated Israel, and the Babylonians defeated Judah. Unified Israel was destroyed and dispersed once again.

Prior to this captivity, the Jew was in control of Canaan land, and Jerusalem was secure. Israel had reached its zenith, its pinnacle of growth, prestige, power, and prosperity. At last, it appeared obedience to God was achieved as the Jews completed the task God had commanded them to do: reenter and conquer the land given to Abraham over four hundred years ago. Freed from Egyptian captivity and forty years in the desert, these second-generation Israelites had conquered the promised land. Their original zest waned however. And within a short period of time, Israel became divided, and God's

Word no longer took priority in the life of the Jews. Their internal and external struggles eventually weakened the divided nation so that captivity of God's people took place again.

The northern kingdom of Israel was made up of ten of the twelve original tribes of Israel. The southern kingdom of Judah consisted of the remaining two tribes. Before captivity, both kingdoms were ruled by separate kings. Both kingdoms were rebellious and disobedient against God. The northern kingdom continuously erred in abominations against God with a lack of open repentance. While Judah sinned too, she was penitent eventually. Consequently, their captivity, both brought about because of rebellion, was quite different. Their captors were distinct one from the other, and the treatment of their Hebrew subjects was distinct. Because the captors were so different, the outcome of the Jews themselves after this particular captivity was very different too. This fact becomes even more important as we parallel the differences within our spiritual makeup.

Assyria was a warring nation, and her culture was geared for conquest. She used deportation and assimilation of her captives into other lands in order to destroy her enemy's culture and heritage. Her method of enemy deportation was recorded first. She removed captives from their homeland and replenished the area with other peoples. Deportation was a means of total conquest as then the captives, and especially their posterity, lost their national identity. The effect that deportation had on Assyria's enemies was tremendous. When nationalism was crushed and the captives were assimilated into Assyrian society, any possible future revolt had been avoided.

The northern kingdom, Israel, fell prey to the cruel oppressor, Assyria. The conquerors deported the Jews back to Assyria and imported foreigners into Israel. All the Jews in the northern kingdom were not deported, but those Jews that were deported were never allowed to return to Israel. The Jews that were removed to Assyria were replaced in Israel by Assyrians themselves and other conquered subjects. Intermarriage was encouraged. The foreigners and the remaining surviving Israelites living within the northern kingdom intermarried and gave rise to the mixed-blooded Jew called the Samaritan. The Assyrian empire eventually fell prey to disintegration, though she had experienced more than one zenith to power.

The geographical location of the Fertile Crescent in Mesopotamia placed this land area in the trade-route crossings of the world. Empire upon empire fell to the onslaught of other people who in return fell to other people. Even today, the Middle East is the hotbed of the world; it is the crossroads between the East and West. Fighting continues.

Following the defeat of the northern kingdom of Israel by Assyria was the defeat of the southern kingdom, Judah, by the Babylonians. The Babylonians were the co-empire during this period of time. They were not as warlike as the Assyrians. In fact, the main recorded military exploit is the one recorded in the Bible during the period of Nebuchadnezzar. The Babylonian had comparatively little interest in war in contrast to their more warring Assyrian neighbors. The treatment of their Judean captives was very different.

The Babylonians allowed their Judean captives to remain segregated upon deportation to Babylon. Thus the seventy-year captivity of the Jews under Babylonian rule found the Hebrew still intact in both culture and heritage. Intermarriage was discouraged, and retaining their own Jewish culture was of paramount importance to the Judeans, which mattered little to their captors. Even though the Jews of the southern kingdom were deported, not all Judeans went to Babylon. Furthermore, other peoples were not moved into the vacated Judean territory. The land remained dormant with a scattering of Jews present.

The Northern Jew was separated from his heritage. The Southern Jew heavily relied upon his heritage to retain continuous fever and zest for return to his homeland. The Davidic line remained intact, and the Jews of the southern kingdom, Judah, continuously believed in their inheritance from God Himself in regard to the coming Messiah from the line of David. Jerusalem was located in the southern kingdom. This fact linked the Judean even closer to his homeland, for the temple was in Jerusalem, the core of all religious activity. After seventy years, according to prophetic utterance, the Judeans were allowed to return to Judah.

> And this whole land shall be a desolation, and an astonishment; and these nations shall serve the king of Babylon seventy years. (Jeremiah 25:11)

> For, lo, the days come, saith the Lord, that I will bring again the captivity of my people Israel and Judah, saith the Lord: and I will cause them to return to the land that I gave to their fathers, and they shall possess it. (Jeremiah 30:3)

The Jewish nation was rebuilt. The prophets continued to exhort and prophesy. Judah remained a nation until history's greatest moment, the birth of Jesus Christ. It wasn't until the Roman defeat of Israel in AD 70 that the Jews were dispersed throughout the world, the Diaspora. We do not see reunification of God's chosen land by his people again until 1948 with the rebirth of a nation—modern Israel. Lying dormant for nearly two thousand years under the dominion of various Gentile rulers, Israel is now risen, resurrected, and a power in the world to be contended with. Israel's final regathering was prophesied even before her Babylonian captivity had taken place.

> And it shall come to pass in that day, that the Lord shall set his hand again the second time to recover the remnant of his people, which shall be left, from Assyria, and from Egypt, and from Pathros, and from Cush, and from Elam, and from Shinar, and from Hamath, and from the islands of the sea. And he shall up and ensign for the nations, and shall assemble the outcasts of Israel, and gather together the dispersed of Judah from the four corners of the earth. (Isaiah 11:11–12)

God's power never ceases to amaze. God's Word is absolute and truth. Everything else varies but not God and His Word!

What significance do these historical facts have to do with the Christian and his inner man? As we have traced the Hebrews' journey from out of Egypt to Jerusalem, we have found that each tribe encountered is a counterpart or type of our inner man. There is an inner story as well as an outer story. With each victory over the seven tribes, our soulish makeup has discovered the absolute truth about man, his base nature. As we conquer Jerusalem and enter into the central core of our being, we are shocked to find that our innermost feeling is totally consumed with self. Just as the Jebusites are the vilest and degenerate of all the tribes, so we find a parallel within our own being. Each tribe that was conquered or each trait that was unclothed relates to our true sin nature. After Jerusalem was conquered or after the sin nature was truly revealed and believed by the Christian, still captivity will periodically come into his life as perfection is not possible, but it is the goal for the believer. We are blind to our own sin nature sometimes and feel once again that we have made self-improvements and self-successes, forgetting that the Father receives all glory. As believers, therefore, we find ourselves in captivity from time to time in order to see ourselves and realize our never-ending need of grace. Grace is God's gift to man as man is never going to rid himself of himself. If he were able to completely overcome self, grace would then be nullified. The giver of grace, Jesus Christ, would be for no purpose. This is, of course, not true, for the flesh cannot attain perfection. As Spirit believers, we are still flesh also. We sin, and our sin carries us into a captivity just as the Jews experienced. The type of captivity we experience depends on our maturity and desire to follow Jesus as a disciple not counting the cost.

The true sin nature of man is that he consistently keeps himself upon the throne. For all his determination and diligence with the Lord, it is still self that looms on the horizon. Our thoughts are upon ourselves as we continually look inward. We are consumed with self. But we are commanded by God to look outward and love our neighbor. We are to meet our neighbor's needs before our own. Without the indwelling power of the Holy Spirit, man is not even aware of his plight. Only God Himself is able to reveal our selfish nature to ourselves. Only God is able to save us.

It would appear that the closer we get to the throne room of God, the better we would feel about ourselves. But in reality, just the opposite is true. For as the Christian taps ever closer to the heartbeat of God, he sees his own unworthiness. His own sin nature in the presence of such holiness stares him in the face. The Christian who desires the ever-deeper walk with God ultimately seeks communion with God above all other things. And communion with God brings us into the reality of His perfection, and thus we see our imperfection. We stand naked in the presence of our Father, seeing ourselves as we are and glimpsing somewhat the magnitude of His love; for such a creature as we really are, His Son died. Oh my God, how humbly we stand. What love you have. It is incomprehensible. Such a Christian stands distraught. What now, Father?

Suddenly, this Christian realizes who he is and what Jesus has done for him. Jesus did not just forgive man for sins but became sin for man. Jesus overcame self in man, for self chokes real life out of us. True enjoyment is not found in serving self but is found in serving others. Dying to self, though painful to the flesh of man, is the strength of the inner man. It is the inner man who is the eternal being. And in dying to self, we give life more abundantly to that part of us that is to live forever. God makes the impossible possible. Jerusalem, or the core of man, is not only conquered but can be inhabited because Jesus Christ has paid the price required for the death of self.

> But he was wounded for our transgressions, he
> was bruised for our iniquities: the chastisement
> of our peace was upon him; and with his stripes
> we are healed. (Isaiah 53:5)

We are not only healed physically but emotionally.

Jesus Christ became sin in order that we, as His children, could be free from the consumption of self. It is self and the perpetuation of self that separates man from God. There is no problem whatsoever in following God's laws and principles if self is not involved. But God's principles and laws dictate death to self. We are commanded to die to self. As we die willingly to self, we live and possess the abundant life. The fruit and gifts of the Spirit flow freely throughout our lives. We have meaning and fulfillment in our existence. If we refuse to die to self, we still die but miss life entirely. Life is a burden to be endured rather than a joyous experience in knowing God who is life. Yet man is unable to die to self. This was Lucifer's sin. It is the sin of the universe, our will versus His will. Rebellion and self are one.

God, in His magnificent plan, sent His only begotten Son to not only die for our sins but to become sin in order that we might no longer live in such chains of self-consumption.

> For he hath made him to be sin for us, who knew
> no sin; that we might be made the righteousness
> of God in him. (2 Corinthians 5:21)

Glory to God, Jesus Christ not only died that we might have forgiveness of sins, but He became sin in that we no longer have to suffer condemnation because of sin. We are His inheritance. After God enters into our spirit and we receive the power of God through the baptism of the Holy Spirit, our internal battle rages. Our flesh, though dead, reacts as if it were alive, and we are in a constant struggle within our two natures.

> I am crucified with Christ: nevertheless I live; yet
> not I, but Christ liveth in me: and the life which I
> now live in the flesh I live by the faith of the Son
> of God, who loved me, and gave himself for me.
> (Galatians 2:20)

It is Jesus Himself who brought sin into captivity and will bring self into captivity as well.

> There is therefore now no condemnation to them
> which are in Christ Jesus, who walk not after the
> flesh, but after the Spirit. (Romans 8:1)

Self is dead and placed upon the cross of Jesus Christ. Self is sin, and Jesus took sin to the cross and became sin so that we no longer have to suffer by sin. This does not imply that we do not sin.

> If we say that we have no sin, we deceive ourselves, and the truth is not in us. (1 John 1:8)

Yet we confess our sins and receive forgiveness.

> If we confess our sins, he is faithful and just to forgive us our sins, and to cleanse us from all unrighteousness. (1 John 1:9)

And as we are free from our sin upon repentance, we must realize too that we cannot rid ourselves of our thoughts of sin. Yet Jesus, because He not only forgives us for sin, but also became sin for us, has already judged our sin and freed us from condemnation by it. It must be remembered that the condemnation toward oneself is sin too. It is at this point that even though we have reached Jerusalem in our own lives and see self as the center core of all our sins, we still find ourselves in captivity periodically, just as the children of Abraham fell to Assyria and Babylonia. Self is not eradicated but covered—covered in the blood of Jesus. And many times, it takes captivity in order for us to realize that the covering is off and that it is repentance of sins and the grace of God that we need.

We can neither cease to think of ourselves, nor can we improve ourselves any more than we have the power to forgive ourselves. All is Jesus Christ. He is the all in all. It bears repeating that dying to self is a process initiated by the Holy Spirit and is under His control and direction. We cannot be in control in any way whatsoever, or we inadvertently will take the credit, as flesh is always there, hoping to receive some glory in any way possible. If flesh is able to see glory in dying, it will join in. Dying is that process where self actually leaves the throne, and Jesus Christ sits in Jerusalem. It is not something to be achieved, it is something gained in loving and worshipping God. The deeper the death, the deeper the pain. But out of pain is glory and resurrection. To such, we are blinded until the process has completed itself. To prefer another over oneself, to keep the preference in secret, to never seek exaltation, to depend utterly on God, is the Jesus-filled life. But only He can give such life to those chosen ones.

Chapter 14

The Outcome

If they sin against thee, (for there is no man
that sinneth not,) and thou be angry with
them, and deliver them to the enemy, so that
they carry them away captives unto the land of
the enemy, far or near; Yet if they shall bethink
themselves in the land whither they were carried
captives, and repent, and make supplication
unto thee in the land of them that carried them
captives, saying, We have sinned, and have done
perversely, we have committed wickedness; And
so return unto thee with all their heart, and with
all their soul, in the land of their enemies, which
led them away captive, and pray unto thee
toward their land, which thou gavest unto their
fathers, the city which thou hast chosen, and the
house which I have built for thy name: Then
hear thou their prayer and their supplication
in heaven thy dwelling place, and maintain
their cause, And forgive thy people that have
sinned against thee and all their transgressions
wherein they have transgressed against thee,
and give them compassion before them who
carried them captive, that they may have

compassion on them: For they be thy people,
and thine inheritance, which thou broughtest
forth out of Egypt from the midst of the
furnace of irons: For thou didst separate them
from among all the people of the earth, to be
thine inheritance, as thou spakest by the hand
of Moses they servant, when thou broughtest
our fathers out of Egypt, O Lord God.

—1 Kings 8:46—51, 53

This then is a principle of God; He allows us to go into captivity to then free us from that which ensnares us. This is a continuous process. We are in the promised land. Captivity is only for a while. And because of our repentance, we always return to the promised land. We are the body of Christ, sons and daughters of the living God of all creation. It is not defeat we have tasted but victory in the fullest sense. Our freedom becomes greater and greater, and it continues to grow as we walk with Jesus Christ and are led by the Spirit of God.

Our freedom is freedom from self. And freedom from self is freedom from inner torment. Self-worship is actually that we have set ourselves up as God Himself. We wish to be God. It is not so much that we wish to control the universe or contend with all the people of the world, doing God's business. It is that we want God's glory, His adoration for ourselves. We wish to be adored and worshipped. Only God is worthy of praise, nothing and no one else.

Thou art worthy, O Lord, to receive glory and
honor and power: for thou hast created all things,
and for thy pleasure they are and were created.
(Revelation 4:11)

How much there is yet to know of Jesus Christ. What He has for His children who love Him first and foremost! Eye has not seen, nor ear heard, neither have entered into the heart of man the things which God hath prepared for them that love him. (1 Corinthians

2:9). We remember that it is Jesus who pulls us out of death. He cleanses us. He fills us. He walks with us. He teaches us. He cares for us. He loves us. He is love. Our life in Him is the priceless pearl, the riches untold, the divine gift of God.

> Have mercy upon me, O God, according to thy lovingkindness: according unto the multitude of thy tender mercies blot out my transgressions. Wash me thoroughly from mine inquity, and cleanse me from my sin. For I acknowledge my transgressions: and my sin is ever before me. Behold, I was shapen in iniquity; and in sin did my mother conceive me. Cast me not away from thy presence; and take not thy Holy Spirit from me. Behold, thou desirest truth in the inward parts: and in the hidden part thou shalt make me to know wisdom. (Psalm 51:1–3, 5, 11, 6)

About the Author

Merritt Lane has been writing for over forty years. Her background includes teaching high school history, running for the state senate, and then establishing her own motivational company: Merritt, People, Quality, Service. She traveled throughout the United States and Canada, presenting seminars to schools, churches, businesses, organizations, and Fortune 500 companies. She also has continued teaching home Bible studies to friends. Merritt and Charlie have been happily married for over fifty-two years. They have two wonderful sons, two lovely daughters-in-law, and eight precious grandchildren.

Printed in the USA
CPSIA information can be obtained
at www.ICGtesting.com
LVHW091207260424
778409LV00001B/251